Praise for
The Comfort Trap, or
What If You're Riding a Dead Horse?

"With warmth, wisdom, a gentle push, and lots of good advice, Dr. Sills invites and inspires us to step into a larger, more gratifying life."
—Harriet Lerner, Ph.D., author of *The Dance of Anger*

"Judith Sills is the voice of clarity, wisdom and common sense that yells 'Enough already' in a way that we can hear and act on her sage advice."
—Joan Borysenko, Ph.D., author of *Inner Peace for Busy Women*

"This book is wise and funny and full of hope. Creative, practical, imaginative and sane, Dr. Sills really knows how to help people get unstuck. She is brilliant, and her book is a sparkling gem."
—Edward Hallowell, M.D., author of *The Childhood Roots of Adult Happiness* and *Driven to Distraction*

"Is there anyone who hasn't loved someone too long, endured a bad situation too often or gotten stuck in a rut of some kind that runs down their self esteem and emotional well being? . . . There is much to learn here—and real tools to use to disengage from unproductive, repeated behaviors that may seem inescapable—but are not. If you are spinning your wheels—this is a book that will give you traction."
—Pepper Schwartz, Ph.D., author of *Everything You Know About Love and Sex Is Wrong*

"A delightful read and a very effective recipe for helping you push through your fears and change what isn't working in your life."
—Susan Jeffers, Ph.D., author of *Feel the Fear and Do It Anyway* and *Embracing Uncertainty*

"Dr. Sills' straightforward vision ⬚⬚⬚⬚⬚⬚ ⬚⬚⬚ ⬚⬚⬚⬚fort zone. This is a book that could ⬚⬚⬚
—Sharon Wohlmuth, coau⬚⬚⬚ ⬚⬚⬚⬚⬚ ⬚ers and *Best Friends*

"Dr. Sills has the solution. Next time you need to talk to the boss, dump the boyfriend, start the diet, get honest with your mom, get control of your finances . . . this is the book that shows you how to dig deep inside, muster the motivation and just do it."

— Julie Morgenstern, author of *Organizing from the Inside Out*

"In this wonderful book, Dr. Sills provides a wide variety of practical and easy-to-understand solutions to those challenges. If you want to bring a sense of joy and balance back to your life, don't pass up this book!"

— Dr. Joseph Mercola, author of the *New York Times* bestseller *The No-Grain Diet* and founder of Mercola.com

"A must-have motivational tool for anyone striving for personal change. . . . I devoured every word."   — Linda Stankard, *BookPage*

"Both inspiring and funny."   — *Psychology Today*

PENGUIN BOOKS

THE COMFORT TRAP

Judith Sills, Ph.D., is the author of the #1 *New York Times* bestseller *Excess Baggage*, as well as *Loving Men More, Needing Men Less, A Fine Romance,* and *How to Stop Looking for Someone Perfect and Find Someone to Love.* A three-year National Science Foundation fellow, Dr. Sills is a contributing editor to *Family Circle* magazine and has written for *O: The Oprah Magazine, Cosmopolitan, Mademoiselle,* and other national magazines. A nationally recognized public speaker and former radio host, she is a clinical psychologist in private practice in Philadelphia.

THE COMFORT TRAP

OR, WHAT IF YOU'RE RIDING A DEAD HORSE?

Judith Sills, Ph.D.

PENGUIN BOOKS

For Larry and Spencer
You are the light that shines on me . . .

PENGUIN BOOKS

Published by the Penguin Group
Penguin Group (USA) Inc., 375 Hudson Street, New York, New York 10014, U.S.A.
Penguin Group (Canada), 10 Alcorn Avenue, Toronto, Ontario, Canada M4V 3B2
    (a division of Pearson Penguin Canada Inc.)
Penguin Books Ltd, 80 Strand, London WC2R 0RL, England
Penguin Ireland, 25 St Stephen's Green, Dublin 2, Ireland (a division of Penguin Books Ltd)
Penguin Group (Australia), 250 Camberwell Road, Camberwell,
    Victoria 3124, Australia (a division of Pearson Australia Group Pty Ltd)
Penguin Books India Pvt Ltd, 11 Community Centre, Panchsheel Park,
    New Delhi–110 017, India
Penguin Group (NZ), cnr Airborne and Rosedale Roads, Albany,
    Auckland 1310, New Zealand (a division of Pearson New Zealand Ltd)
Penguin Books (South Africa) (Pty) Ltd, 24 Sturdee Avenue, Rosebank,
    Johannesburg 2196, South Africa

Penguin Books Ltd, Registered Offices: 80 Strand, London WC2R 0RL, England

First published in the United States of America by Viking Penguin,
a member of Penguin Group (USA) Inc. 2004
Published in Penguin Books 2005

10   9   8   7   6   5   4   3   2   1

Grateful acknowledgment is made for permission to reprint an excerpt from "Moon River"
by Johnny Mercer and Henry Mancini. © 1960 Famous Music Corporation (ASCAP).
All rights reserved. Used by permission.

THE LIBRARY OF CONGRESS HAS CATALOGED THE HARDCOVER EDITION AS FOLLOWS:
Sills, Judith.
The comfort trap or, what if you're riding a dead horse? / Judith Sills.
p.   cm.
Includes index.
ISBN 0-670-85847-1 (hc.)
ISBN 0 14 30.3455 3 (pbk.)
1. Self-efficacy.   2. Change (Psychology)   3. Self-actualization (Psychology)   I. Title.
BF637.S38S55 2004
158.1—dc22   2003062450

Printed in the United States of America

CONTENTS

AUTHOR'S NOTE

Some years ago, back at the dawn of Prozac, I met weekly with a woman who was excruciatingly single and full of self-recrimination for it. Hers is a familiar unhappy story. Our sessions centered on dates to which she brought an excess of hope; the relationships ended with just enough of a twist that she could never seem to learn from one in order to cushion the disappointment of the next.

She and I spent two years together in this loop: focused from man to man, from possibility to pain, with no particular positive learning curve that either of us could observe. During this time she completed an advanced degree, found a better than decent job in her field, and bought a home. She didn't delight in these achievements because they were not her true heart's desire.

Still, I pointed to these accomplishments frequently, wondering why in our huge, rich universe of possibilities, marriage was her only path to satisfaction. It was, though, and she had no genuine interest in art or music, politics or travel, literature or architecture, or Rollerblading or anything else on this planet except meeting a man and getting married. That's not to say that she didn't participate in much of the above. She did, but dutifully, to become the woman she needed to be so that a suitable man would love her. Her pastimes were just that, passing time. Her only passion was for a relationship.

Eventually, she got worse. A broken engagement precipitated a more acute depression, killing her appetite, interrupting her sleep, and holding the black gun of despair to her head. As a clinical psychologist I do not prescribe medication, so I referred her to the psychiatrist with whom I consult. I saw her on a Tuesday; he met with her on Wednesday and gave her a prescription for Prozac. We spoke several times and met ten days later. When I saw her, this is what she said:

"A funny thing happened on the way to your office. I stopped at the bookstore to buy the new *Cosmopolitan*, but when I picked it up, it didn't look interesting to me. Instead, for some weird reason, I wanted to read *U.S. News & World Report*. That's what I bought." She took it out of the bag and showed it to me.

Ten days on medication, and she was changed.

From that moment, and in so many ways, she was unarguably different. Not only different, but in her opinion, and in mine, she was better. It wasn't simply that her depression was largely gone, though it was. It was that something else was gone, her narrowness of thinking, her conviction that there was only one path to happiness, her rigid, entrenched apathy. Gone. It was as if a switch was thrown and this lovely, sad, struggling woman had come to life.

The change persisted. An unfamiliar sense of optimism.

Travel plans. Fun at work. Giggling over dates in a complete absence of desperation. She got interested in writing. Turned down an attractive man because she was going to a writer's conference. Went and had a good time. Damn it. She was Sleeping Beauty and Prozac was the prince's kiss.

That was my first experience with the way in which medication can—only rarely, unpredictably, often only temporarily—make the dead horse simply vanish in the night. This experience changed my thinking forever about causes, cures, and my own role in both. It might change you.

In my practice I have seen this profound reaction occur only rarely, whether to Prozac or its several descendants. Perhaps for every ten of my patients who have a trial of medication—prescribed by either my consulting psychiatrist or their own physician—only one person has experienced this penetrating and life-altering release from a prison of emotional pain. The other nine people have experienced a range of reactions from significant improvement, through modest gains, down to no help at all. Some have felt unpleasant side effects and a few have experienced frightening and seriously destabilizing upheavals. These pills are no magic bullet; their positive effects sometimes inexplicably evaporate and the risks are real.

Still, the person who swallows a few pills and is suddenly different in some desirable way is experiencing change of a different order of magnitude. I don't know if you would be that person. I don't know if you need to be or want to be, if you'd choose the risks involved, or even where you stand on the philosophical questions such pills naturally generate.

What follows from here is a book about getting yourself to change—about why, where, and how you might move yourself forward in your life. The book talks about the part you can do, will have to do, on your own. Let's face it, your part is most of it, pill or no pill.

But just as psychotherapy is a resource for change, medication is a resource, too. I won't mention it again, but I want you to remember it's out there.

Judith Sills, Ph.D.
February 22, 2003

THE COMFORT TRAP

OR, WHAT IF YOU'RE

RIDING A

DEAD HORSE?

CHAPTER 1

THE MAN IN THE
BLACK MERCEDES

A re you up for a fight?

Because I'm telling you, right up front, it's a fight to get from where you are to what you want. That battle is with yourself.

We are the rocks we are pushing uphill—if and when we choose to make the push. Most of the time we don't. Why not? What makes it such a struggle to push ourselves even when we are pushing ourselves toward something better? It's difficult because, however unsatisfying it is where we are, *it is also comfortable*.

In the high-wire act that is life, most of our time is spent huddled on a comfortable platform of our own creation. We could stay safely snuggled there—busy, preoccupied, suffering, or delighted. It is a familiar and confining harbor, and its only exit is a tightrope stretched to the next safe haven. Eventually, uncomfortably, the spotlight of promise moves to that next platform and our own grows painful or empty. When it does, we freeze in place. Can we risk that tightrope of change?

What will you do?

Many will look determinedly away from the tightrope. Who knows, after all, where it leads? Some few will fling themselves forward, while others will inch out and back and farther out again, making wobbly, determined progress toward the light. Most will listen as hard to their audience as to their own hearts, drawing courage or caution from the chorus around them.

Of those who risk the tightrope, we know for certain some will fall. The rest will make it to a new platform, larger, richer, more satisfying than the old one. They will bring with them both an enduring pride for having made the leap and a degree of pain from their loss of what was left behind. Much of what was left behind were people who were unable or unwilling to make a similar vault. They stayed stuck. What about you?

Frankly, most of us will linger on the platform of our comfort zone forever, unless it collapses beneath us and life forces us onto the tightrope. If it does, we suffer and eventually savor the pleasures of change. But without that push it can be a very long wait for those pleasures—until you get enough money, or meet the right person, or lose the weight; until the kids leave home, or you finally get fired, or your parents die, or your mate leaves you so you don't bear the guilt for doing the leaving. In the meantime, your platform holds and holds you to it, and life becomes a summer rerun, if only because you feel unable to create a brand-new episode.

There are the few who show us a different way, who turn their backs on familiar comfort and rush toward the tightrope with breathtaking confidence, propelled by a passionate conviction.

Of course, these people tend to be known as either saints or madmen—Gandhi or Golda Meir, Nelson Mandela or Larry Kramer—and you are probably neither, so what is there to learn from them? We have other contemporary figures who lingered on a comfortable platform of conventional beliefs and then, through some personal epiphany, took a leap across to a higher plane. I think of Oskar Schindler or Rosa Parks or Anwar Sadat as three examples, though you may consider them to be saints or madmen, too.

These are historic figures, legends even, whose stories dramatize deliberate personal change writ large. There are other stories of risk and success that guide us on a more human scale. These people show us how to move forward deliberately, consciously, to expand the platforms of our comfort zone, to stretch that platform bit by bit, always pushing into new territory, gnawing away at our boundaries and opening up our possibilities.

Think of Oprah—not white, not thin, not connected, not cherished, and not letting any of this stop her on her Sherman's march to the microphone. Think of Madonna—who meets every success with the next risk, who often fails and has yet to falter. Hell, think of Scarlett—who saw opportunity in a pair of curtains and postponed her fears until tomorrow, which is when most of us schedule the risk of change. These are people who make life happen, rather than waiting to see what happens.

What about you? Could you step out on that limb, past propriety, past security, past your own familiar sense of yourself? Could you confront the bully, risk the rejection, open the business, leave the marriage, insist on the raise, take up tap dancing, disappoint your father, go back to school, face disapproval, learn to ski at your age, hit on the lifeguard or even the president—

assuming you'd want to, of course. Could you break your own boundaries because something you want to have or someone you want to be is on the other side?

I think of the title of a 1950s autobiography, *I Leap Over the Wall*, when I am working with someone who is longing to change something in his or her life but feels utterly unable to proceed. As I recall, the book told the story of a nun and her struggle to leave the convent, but to me the title suggested the emotional effort so many of us make in our attempt to move life in a positive direction. From the grand inspiration of Meir or Mandela to the merely social aspirations of Wallis Simpson, moving in on the Duke, all leapt over some wall.

The Comfort Trap or, What If You're Riding a Dead Horse? is about that wall and how to leap over it when it's standing in your way. It may be the wall in your marriage that prohibits you from saying all the things you'd like to say. It may be the wall that keeps you in a professional pit, soothing yourself by identifying with all the fellow wallowers who are keeping you company. It may be the barrier between you and a physically healthy life, a barrier composed of all your self-destructive, deliciously satisfying impulses. The wall is made of fear and habit, and the energy required to scale it is considerable. The thing is, much of what you want in life is on the other side.

The Comfort Trap or, What If You're Riding a Dead Horse? is a guide to wall leaping. The principles of forward motion are the same whether what is on the other side of your personal wall is more money, profound intimacy, a sense of purpose, or a divorce. This is a book about crossing your own boundaries in order to move forward in life.

This book centers on the paradox of the psychological comfort zone. We need to be comfortable to live fully, yet if we're too comfortable, something essential dies. A life that is too much work erodes the body, but one that requires too little effort depletes the soul. Between these two poles there is a harbor, a state of psychological grace, a platform of emotional well-being. It is your comfort zone. It is a haven. And, by its very nature, it is temporary.

Your current comfort zone includes the familiar, tolerable, and therefore safe circumstances you have created in your life. For some period these circumstances—your job, your affair, your passion for bridge, your neighborhood, your friendship circle, your marriage—may be intensely satisfying. When satisfaction is added to safety, your comfort zone functions exactly as intended. It becomes a psychological greenhouse where you can flower, thrive, and contribute something back to the world.

At some point, however, every comfort zone diminishes in satisfaction. The job ceases to challenge or the management no longer supports you; the marriage hits a logjam of conflict and disappointment; the old friend exploits your generosity yet another time; the excitement of dating devolves into the chore of selection; the passion of the affair becomes the poison of guilt; and the nice girl is still sitting around, waiting to meet her Duke.

Over and over we will return to this same theme: Comfort is pleasure plus safety, satisfaction colored with security. There are intense satisfactions—deeply honest relationships, sexual thrills, athletic feats, great goals—which can only be delivered in the absence of security. These satisfactions can only be achieved beyond the boundaries of one's comfort zone, though, and that is the point. Comfort is charismatic precisely because it is safe—and therein lies its power. But safety limits the amount of satisfaction any experience can deliver—and therein lies its painful limitation.

Our comfort zones are constructed from utterly idiosyncratic elements, but some structural features are universal. Comfort is physical, of course. Before your spirit registers its vote, comfort begins with your body. And much of comfort is contrast, lost over time when the sharpness of relief disappears. Comfort is a fire when you are in from the cold and a fan when you are escaping the heat. It is knowing you have sisters who would lay down their lives for you but not seeing too much of them over the holidays. Comfort is rest after effort, but not endless rest. It is relief after risk, but not eternal safety—because eternal safety stops being satisfying.

Identifying the physical aspect of comfort is easy because, after all, we know what feels good. But the essence of comfort is something emotional, and that is not so simple. Emotional comfort is the feeling of "fit," and we seek it as instinctively and cherish it as passionately as we seek love and value money. But unlike love and money, which are publicly professed ideals, we do not celebrate our quest for comfort. Sometimes we don't even realize it.

First and foremost, emotional fit is established by habit and routine. Routine defines us, carving our lives into little mini-zones of emotional comfort—my coffee shop, my preference for black, one Sweet'N Low not Equal please, my parking spot, my nightly ritual of walking the dog or stalking the bars. The soothing balm of routine defines and confines us all. We *always do what we always did*, unless we make a conscious, focused, and often formidable effort not to. This is true whether what we did felt good or bad, because in some essential way it feels like me. It fits.

Fit is only partly defined by the complex matrix of your routine. It is also powerfully influenced by the sweeping psychological concept of identity. You and I have a rigidly etched idea of who we are. That idea is huge, pervasive, and probably only partly understood, but its power over our lives cannot be overstated.

We are largely the people we expect to be, because that identity shapes the way we sort through the thousand life choices with which we are confronted daily. Sometimes, though, those old familiar choices can leave us suddenly stuck.

Identity's enormous influence over how we act explains why the man who believes he will be the boss's favorite probably will be, while the woman who believes men only want her for sex finds over and over again that men only want her for sex; the man whose managers never appreciate him re-creates his experience of being undervalued in job after job with no sense of his own contribution to the process, while the woman who cannot leave her high-paying job to have a better time is correct when she explains that she cannot.

"Whether you think you can or think you can't, you're right," goes the saying. Your identity defines whether you think you can or think you can't, and those thoughts then delineate the boundaries of your current comfort zone. Change those boundaries and you will certainly change what you think. Change what you think about who you are and you will profoundly change your life.

Frankly, why bother? Why make such an effort to think differently, to be someone new or act in a way other than you usually do? Because as comfortable as those behaviors are, they limit you. If what you want to achieve or who you want to be is inside the zone of your identity or your habits, you are, at least temporarily, content. Eventually, though, what once made you content may now afford you little uplift, and possibly a good deal of sorrow.

What to do? Well, that would seem obvious enough. Leave. Move on. Stir things up. Quit. Focus elsewhere. Start something new. Make a change. If what you are doing is no longer working, do something else. If the horse is dead, get off.

Except, sometimes we don't. Can't. Won't. Don't know how. Aren't sure we should. Don't know where to go next. Can't break the rule that says we shouldn't go there.

Or, you know perfectly well what you should do, but you can't seem to get yourself to do it. Hate yourself for your inadequacy, mourn the price of your anxiety, but still you stay put. Not entirely sure of what is holding you in place but unable to move forward under your own steam. Stuck in your comfort zone.

Stuck

"I'm stuck," said the shiny man sitting across from me. His hair, product-tamed and light-reflecting, matches a remarkable pair of gleaming loafers. I get a first impression of a glossy hardback novel squashed between classy bookends.

The man between these bookends is Jack and he has come to see me because he is sad. Unremittingly, and worse, work-inhibitingly sad and stuck, since his girlfriend of five years left him last month. Jane left because Jack won't marry her, and he's come to see me because he fears that this time—the third time she's left—she might not come back. This time he fears that if he wants her, he will have to take a step forward. And the fact is, he can't.

Jack is deeply attached to Jane, loves her, longs for her, and doesn't want to face life without her, or so he explains to me at his first visit, going on in some detail about the wonders of Jane until he is reassured that I understand the problem is not with Jane, nor is it with love. The problem is something else, something he can't quite grasp, although it is costing him dearly.

Jack is caught in his comfort zone and marriage is on the other side of his mental fence. When Jane keeps him company where he is, Jack is a wondrously content, shiny man. But when she insists, for reasons of her own, on moving the relationship forward, he is emotionally unable to follow. So Jack mourns his loss and pursues Jane with passion, desperate to pull her back to where he is stuck. Twice before he has been able to do this, albeit only temporarily.

This time Jack has come to me looking for a way out of his conflict, although he frames his request differently. "I need to make a decision," he says. "I love Jane, but I don't see myself married. Well, maybe someday, but not now, not yet."

I squint. Jack is forty-one. I don't think timing or age is the issue.

Jack continues. If he's so uncertain about marriage, doesn't that perhaps suggest that Jane is not the right woman, that certain shortcomings of hers, too trivial to mention but irritating nonetheless, may be true emotional barriers? Perhaps it's best that he let Jane go or she him? Perhaps, if love is this hard, it really isn't love?

I glance at my watch. Good. In twenty-five minutes we have gone from "it's not about Jane" to "could it be it's all about Jane?" Jack is open, expressive, and we may be able to move fairly quickly to the part that has to do with Jack.

He begins to talk about marriage—the wonderful marriage his parents had and what was awful about it, the tedious marriages of his friends and what he dreads from those. Finally, at the end of our first meeting, Jack shared with me his personal vision, the internal image he treasures.

"Maybe I actually saw this man, or maybe I made him up," Jack said. "But I call him the Man in the Black Mercedes. He is the man I've always wanted to be. He lives alone in a small, elegant house filled with art. He has a houseman who handles the maintenance and a housekeeper who tends to his personal chores. He dates exotic women, loves one or two, enjoys his work, and makes enough money to afford this life because, after all, he's only spending it on himself. He has a hundred friends, entertains them lavishly, gets invited everywhere.

"The Man in the Black Mercedes treats the woman in his life very well, but he doesn't live with her. He maintains a certain boundary. If you ask him why he doesn't marry, he'll say, 'I'm single not because I want to sleep with many women, but because I want to be free to sleep alone when I choose to.'

"If I marry Jane," Jack concludes, "I'll never be the Man in the Black Mercedes." By holding on to his long-standing reluctance to marry, Jack is making an old, familiar, comfortable choice. But now it doesn't offer the old familiar satisfaction.

In my twenty-five years as a psychotherapist I have met the Man in the Black Mercedes many times, in many forms. He is an internal icon of perfect, static contentment, the universal fantasy that everything and everyone we need is inside our magic circle and none of them has conflicting needs of his own. We are at once perfectly safe and perfectly satisfied.

But Jack is no longer perfectly satisfied. Now he is only safe.

Jack's safety is hard to enjoy without Jane to love and be loved by. It's painful safety, too, because he's threatened with the loss of Jane and that will be a genuine heartache. But in order to follow her, Jack has to leave the safety of his comfort zone, his carefully constructed, well-defended, emotionally even life.

To move forward toward satisfaction, Jack would have to risk his safety with no guarantee of how he'll feel in the future, despite Jane's many reassurances. He would have to launch himself on the dangerous raft of attachment and navigate the white waters of marriage and family. What if she is the wrong person? What if he wants off later, when it's too late? What if something permanent happens—a child, a joint bank account—to put the Man in the Black Mercedes out of reach forever? Forward is too dangerous. Staying here is too sad. Stuck.

Jack's paralysis might be familiar to you. Perhaps the air in your own life has grown stale, or worse. What was once motivating has turned mysteriously flat, done with. Your life has run out of soul and there is no obvious refueling station.

You cannot see your way out of a situation and you can no longer bear to be in it. Something is missing or the world is too much with you; you have profoundly disappointed yourself or you don't feel much of anything at all. There is a next step forward, you've been assured, but you can't see it. Or perhaps you can see it, but getting there is another story.

This dead end takes so many forms:

It's the job you can't leave, though it's sucking your life dry, because where else are you going to make this kind of money?

It's the alcoholic or rageoholic or shopoholic mate you can't leave, because you are too afraid of being alone.

It's the club you can't join, the trip you can't take, the success you can't enjoy, because the new people seem so different from your old friends.

It's the parallel lives you and your mate have constructed to avoid each other, because you don't feel you can confront the issues in your marriage.

It's any important relationship—friend, parent, sibling, adult child, lover, spouse—whose demands exhaust and infuriate you, but any attempt to insist on reciprocity threatens to end the connection.

It's the person who is never going to love you back the right way, though you keep imagining how good it would be if he or she did.

It's the job you won't try for, the clothes you won't wear, the sport you wouldn't attempt, because you feel inadequate.

It's Mr. or Ms. Nice, to whom you cannot commit because it would be settling, but whom you cannot leave because what if this is your last chance?

It's the perilous balance you are trying to maintain between the affair you cannot abandon and the marriage that forms the scaffolding of your life.

It's the employee you can't fire, the raise you can't insist on, the credit you can't claim, because you're too uncomfortable with confrontation.

It's the necessary condition—financial stability, weight loss, promotion, falling in love, getting organized—that must occur before you can get what you want, but you can't seem to achieve that necessary condition.

It's your obsessive preoccupation with your ex or some other past injury that interferes with your ability to focus on or take pleasure in the present.

Finally, it's an inner numbness. When your days feel like long jogs on the hamster wheel and you can't see your way off, you're stuck.

When you are loitering at one of these dead ends, think of yourself as being locked into a comfort zone. That's the first step toward making a break for it.

The Invisible Electric Fence: Anxiety

Here's the fine print on comfort: It comes with an invisible electric fence. Keep well away from pushing your own limits and you will be cheerfully oblivious to the walled platform you have created. But stretch out past your zone and you will get a jolt of anxiety that will certainly get your attention. At the very least, when speaking out in the meeting where you usually only look down, or standing up to the bully to whom you had always said, "Yes, dear," the anxiety you feel will give you pause. At its worst, it will keep you from even contemplating quitting or moving or marrying or divorcing or any other "-ing" that is just on the other side of your cozy niche.

Anxiety is the invisible fence that bounds all of our lives. It is what we would do almost anything to avoid. Anxiety is the opposite of comfort and, when it comes to change, it is the heart of the matter. We always do what we always did *because doing something new doesn't usually feel good.* "New" may feel anything from slightly strange to agonizing, but these are all flavors of anxiety.

Yes, there are those among us who have come to savor some forms of anxiety—thrill-seekers for whom the physical spurts of adrenaline seem to stir pleasure centers in their brains and drive them to dangle off cliffs and scream cheerfully on roller coasters. But clearly that does not mean that these hardy spirits are exempt from all forms of anxiety. The fact is, none of us is exempt.

The invisible fence around each of our current lives is highly individual. That's why your best friend could mouth the words "I love you" to a strange man in a bar in a moment of high spirits, but has not been able to leave the man who bores and burdens her. (She can flirt with the thrill of freedom, but separation from a safe relationship paralyzes her.) That's why your mother-in-law is a powerhouse at her church but she'd starve before she ate in a restaurant alone. (When people know and respect her, she's energized, but without that social support she struggles with unaccountable shame.) That's why your brother can make cold calls but he won't enjoy a party full of strangers. (He has numbed himself to telephone rejection through repeated exposure, but face-to-face interpersonal risk overwhelms him.)

OK, but so what? You can go through life quite happily without eating alone or being bored by a roomful of strangers. And frankly there's a lot to be said for a safe, reliable relationship. If it costs you thrills, well, freedom has a high price, too. All of these reservations are perfectly reasonable.

Remember, *there is no more inherent value in pushing the envelope than there is in finding satisfaction with the status quo*. In fact, it's probably more spiritually challenging, more emotionally demanding to find satisfaction where you are than to keep moving from source to source looking for a hit of pleasure. In this sense, the ability to establish a long-term, stable comfort zone and to continue to find satisfaction in it is a mark of emotional maturity.

To a point. Right up to the point of pain. Right up to the dead end. Right up to the moment when you see clearly that there is something you want and it's on the other side of the fence. Between where you are and what you want is the invisible fence of anxiety. How do you scale it?

Well, maybe you won't have to. Sometimes all that's required is going along for the ride.

The Tides of Change

When what you want to experience or the person you want to become is outside your comfort zone, you will be, at least temporarily, stuck. How to exert that titanic effort of will, how to
summon the sheer grit required to face anxiety when you could
relax into a comfortable state of tedium? Quite often, you won't
have to summon that force from within. Life itself exerts that
force on us.

When your life first runs aground, you will probably linger,
waiting for the tide of events to move you forward. We wait for
love to find us; wait in hope that the killer boss will resign or that
more money will make the work more interesting; wait for the
marriage to improve when the financial stress eases or the baby
sleeps through the night; wait and push fiercely for someone else
to change and so make us happier.

Sometimes outside events do solve our problems or at least
change them for a new set. People do meet and fall in love and
everything really does change. Sometimes the boss leaves, morale
soars, and, thank God, you stuck it out. Sometimes the alcoholic
spouse dries out, the selfish one has an emotional awakening. If
your timing is good, if you're lucky or necessary to someone else's
comfort, then the flow of life—in the form of graduation, marriage, childbirth, promotion, a geographic move, an empty nest,
or mandatory retirement—will move you along its river, flinging
you from your comfort zone into new circumstances.

True, some of us resist these developmental tides, refusing the
promotion, turning away from romantic commitment or parent-

hood or even a new home or a career change. When we say no to these new platforms, we do so for good and bad reasons. But at some point or other most of us say yes to some of them and then our choice forces us from our comfort zones and through the invisible fence of anxiety.

The forces that propel us from our nests are not all developmental and certainly not all positive. Every American alive on September 11, 2001, experienced the destruction of our national comfort zone with savage abruptness, and so suffered the grief and fear and rage that always accompanies ruthless change. That was a historic expulsion from safety into something cold and hard, and we will struggle for some time, maybe forever, as we create a new national comfort zone in which to pledge allegiance.

The negative forces that cast us from comfort do not have to be so universal or so sweeping. Accident, illness, death, unwanted divorce, downsizing, all rip us from lives that seem immeasurably comfortable when viewed from atop their wreckage. In these wrenching life upheavals, we are thrown up against the fence of our fears in an emotionally weakened state, which is part of what makes them so horrific to endure. We do endure them, though at a cost.

When life changes us, one way or another we make ourselves comfortable with that change. The ferocious anxiety, that discomfort, the sense of ill fit or of being an imposter that accompanies this surge forward, lasts as long as it lasts. Eventually the new role becomes you, the new job is mastered, the new house becomes home, and you have stretched to create a new comfort zone with its own emotional attachments, its own soothing routines, and its own sources of satisfaction.

In other words, we change pretty much because life forces us to. Things begin, so we adapt (unless we avoid the new beginning). Things end, so we change (unless we find a way to prolong the ending). This is an excellent system as far as it goes.

In your life, it may not have gone far enough. Maybe the prince hasn't come—or worse, he came and left. Maybe the career toward which you were so carefully nudged turned out to be socially acceptable quicksand and no one is throwing you a rescue branch. Your in-laws may never approve of your table manners nor excuse you from Sunday supper. Your marriage is a miserable stalemate, but your kids are young and cheerfully oblivious. Maybe your life will just keep on keepin' on, full of the same complaints and simmering frustrations, a small powerboat on a big ocean with no one at the helm, plowing its vacant course until it runs out of gas. You just can't count on life to put you someplace new, and if it does, the new it chooses might make the old look good.

So we are faced with a dilemma. How do we do the choosing ourselves? How do we force ourselves against that wall of anxiety of our own free will? How do we actually get ourselves to act—to marry this woman, leave this job, refuse to have this baby, divorce this partner, open this business—when the possible painful consequences of these actions are so real and our certainty is so slim?

That's a tricky "how to," but it must be done and the best of us do it again and again. No one does it immediately, few do it easily, and every one of us looks back and notes where we could have been bolder or should have been more cautious. Nevertheless, some of us do eventually act. We decide, despite uncertainty. We move, despite the pain of what is left behind. We act, despite the grave discomfort of action. We create change.

To break the boundaries of your comfort zone, you have to steer in the direction of your own anxiety, step on some inner reserve of psychic fuel, and force yourself across your own boundary. It can be done—in fact, it must be done. And the truth is, people do it all the time. If not you, then who? But if you, well, how?

Several years ago I wrote a book called *Excess Baggage*, about getting out of your own way. It generated some complimentary mail and one very articulate and cynical letter. The letter was from a colleague I'd never met, who described herself as a psychotherapist of some thirty years' experience. My book was very wise, she said, and she had no objection to any of my suggestions for creating a better life. But she herself had been making these suggestions to patients for years, and frankly, her patients made these same suggestions to themselves with great frequency, easily identifying what they should do to improve their lives. The thing is, they hardly ever did what they knew they should. Surely I must have some magic power that gets people to do what I'm suggesting they do, and would I kindly share that?

Ouch. It's perfectly true that what's wrong with self-help—well, with any help for that matter—is that identifying what to do is far easier than getting yourself to do it. But it is possible to get yourself to do it, possible to motivate yourself to change and to sustain that motivation through all the inevitable setbacks and fatigue. Possible and even probable, if you know how to push your own rock all the way up that hill.

I have thought about that letter for years as I've watched what techniques actually help people move themselves past the points where they are stuck, past their own self-limiting anxiety and onto higher ground. *The Comfort Trap or, What If You're Riding a Dead Horse?* is my answer to that letter.

The glory of self-propelled change—whether you want to stop smoking, stand up to your mother, get yourself back to school or out of it once and for all—is that you do not have to find all the energy, day after day, to confront the invisible fence of anxiety on your own. True, you must tote the burden of your fear and your ambivalence and the inevitable pain of loss up some psychological mountain. But the trick is to give this burden a little shove over the edge of your psychic cliff so it will tumble onto new ground of its own momentum, carrying you along with it. That little shove—in the form of one small step outside your comfort zone—will set in motion all the other changes to which you aspire.

In other words, if you're in a dull job, you have to fire yourself; in a stale relationship, you need to dump yourself; in a self-destructive pattern, deprive yourself. If you are afraid to speak, you need to reveal one truth; afraid to hear the answers, you'll need to blurt out a scary question. You will need to create those life circumstances that would have rescued you if only they had come along.

What's going to make you, or anyone else, go to these extremes? For all the sensible, satisfying reasons why we *should* challenge our own limits, there are only two reasons why we will: because we are suffering where we are and/or because we hunger for something that is just over our psychological horizon.

That's pretty much it. Either something comes into your life and you have to get comfortable with it, or you will make yourself deliberately uncomfortable for a damned good reason. The best reason of all is that, when you look around with honest eyes, you realize that the horse is dead. The next chapter describes how you can get off.

CHAPTER 2

SEVEN STEPS

I t's been three years since her divorce, but Ellie continues to cling to the remnants of her married life—same town, same house, same faces at Thanksgiving dinner, minus the one central figure, of course. She contends that she's maintained her old routine for the sake of the children, and that's true as far as it goes. But the rest of the truth is that fear and pain have driven her into a stifling cocoon and she has not been able to find her way out.

Michael knows he is dodging a promotion that should be the next move on his career track. He felt exactly the same way at age ten, when he hated to leave his old neighborhood, and again at eighteen, when he wouldn't consider an out-of-town college. This time, his lover is impatient, his boss is insistent, and Michael himself is not sleeping.

The job as an exotic dancer was intended to finance Diane's ambition to be her family's first college graduate. The money is indeed amazing, but Diane has yet to enroll in her first college course. Somehow she can't see herself fitting in.

James's wife won't have sex. He spoons up at night and finds a pillow jammed between them; reaches to hug her and feels her straining away, waiting for release. She won't discuss her distance, won't tell him what's wrong, won't tell him much of anything else either. The pilot light is out in the marriage and nothing he has tried will reignite it. Lately he is dreaming of dying. When he's awake, James is thinking the impossible: Maybe he should leave.

When her son began college, Ruth, for many years a single mom, finally turned her attention to herself. She lost twenty-eight pounds, had her teeth whitened and her hair highlighted, and went on a blind date. Then something clicked off in her head and she did not do one single other thing to meet a man. Deeply disappointed in herself, Ruth regained the weight and returned to her long-established routine of office work, housework, television, and cookies for company.

Ryan has an attitude. He is way too special for his family's packaging business, though it is worth way too much money to walk away from.

Lydia says she's been "stuck in a rut so long she's starting to furnish it," but she isn't laughing when she says it.

Frances can't bring herself to leave the drunk with whom she lives, though she no longer daydreams about how he's going to change.

Helen is lonely and socially disconnected, but she won't join a club where "everyone looks like they've known each other forever" and she's sure she will be the unwelcome outsider.

And Mercedes Man Jack feels paralyzed, still unable to envision marriage to Jane comfortably, and painfully unhappy without her.

Unfailingly urbane, Jack conducts his psychotherapy sessions like a mildly flirtatious business lunch between colleagues from competing companies. He spends his time fending me off by winning me over. Jack is very far away, hard for me to connect with.

Despite their many profound differences, each of these men and women will need to use a similar method in order to move toward more satisfaction. Wildly divergent as each of their situations is, *they will be resolved through a common path.* And so will yours.

To break through the crust of a comfort zone, to extricate yourself from that safe, stale platform and travel successfully across the tightrope, you and each of the people described will go through a seven-step process. Briefly, here are your steps:

1. **Face What Hurts:** What is painful, missing, unsatisfying, stifling, or frustrating about your current comfort zone? How can you stop distracting yourself from that pain so you can use it to improve your life? Distractions are usually some form of avoidance, blame, fantasy, or denial—the most common ways we try temporarily to ease emotional pain without having to confront change.

2. **Create a Vision:** Where could you go from here? What goal, hope, or possibility might you go toward? Where do you want to end up? How can you create a realistic vision of a new comfort zone, given all your conflicting fears and desires?

3. **Make a Decision:** Just because you are unsatisfied or frustrated doesn't mean it's time to give up. How do you

decide when it's time to move on? How do you know if
the horse is dead?

4. **Identify Your Pattern:** Have you done this before? Your
current situation occurs in a context. What can an examination of your history and personality pattern reveal
about what you need to do next?

5. **Let Go:** What is holding you in place? What guilt, obligation, or attachment must be loosened or resolved before you can move forward? What losses will you incur
and how can you minimize them?

6. **Face Your Fear:** Between your comfort zone and your
heart's desire is the electric fence of anxiety we discussed in Chapter One. Naming, facing, and overcoming
that anxiety is an unavoidable and necessary step along
your way.

7. **Take Action:** What do you need to do to get from here to
there? Change requires action. To leave your comfort
zone and move forward, you will inevitably need to say
something, do something, choose something new. What
kind of script, structure, or support will help you change?
I've listed this as the seventh step, but as you'll see, outside action accompanies internal movement every step
along your way.

That's it. Recognize where you are stuck and what got you
there. Identify what you want that's outside your zone. Decide if
it's the right time to act. Loosen up on the attachments that hold
you back and stretch across your fear to reach your desire.

We'll review this process in great detail through the rest of this
book, so you'll have a clear idea of how to apply it to your own
situation. Keep in mind that, although I've laid this out as seven

steps, this is not precisely a linear process. Rather, these universal steps occur as unfolding stages of changed awareness, clarified feeling, hard decision making, and tolerable risk. Each step forward deepens your understanding of the questions that came before, which in turn strengthens your ability to go farther down the road toward change. The process of deliberately leaving a comfort zone is something of an upward spiral, with each phase influencing the earlier ones and those yet to come.

In fact, while each of the seven steps is a necessary part of the process, you may experience them in an order different from the one I've described. The passage through these stages is that fluid, that overlapping. For example, some people spend a fair amount of time Identifying a Pattern before they are able to Make a Decision, while others handle the process in the reverse order. Likewise, the emotional work of Letting Go or Facing Fear might begin earlier in your own challenge to your comfort zone. The order just described is simplest to understand and the one I've most commonly observed, but your own might take you on a different ride.

So, though I will discuss these unfolding phases in a seemingly orderly fashion, you will probably live them as we all do — in a two steps forward, one step back muddle, with lots of scratching around and following false trails. Don't be discouraged. If you think you are going around in circles for a while, you are probably doing things right.

The fact is, life changes our circumstances all the time. But to take the helm and deliberately change your life involves a different level of decision making and brave action. It calls on your highest self, your focus, discipline, and energy. It requires valuing your connections to others as highly as you cherish your own satisfactions, and sometimes making agonizing choices between them. It costs the protection of some of your most cherished illusions. And it takes courage.

By way of highlighting just how circuitous and individual the route might be through these seven universal steps, here's the story of how Jack found his way home.

A Day at the Beach

"I love Jane, and she knows it. I just don't want to get married," says Jack.

"So your lunch with the Fresh Fields lady [as we refer to his latest flirtation] shouldn't upset her?" I ask.

"Look, I can have lunch with anyone. We're not married."

There is the perfect little traffic circle around which Jack and I are spinning. Here's how he eventually exited. We began, as you will begin when you break free of your own comfort zone, with this first step:

Face What Hurts

What hurts is usually uncomplicated when we look it square in the eye. (We don't, of course, because it hurts.) Jack dodges the hard truth that he can't have a happy Jane (or possibly any Jane at all) *and* his comfortable independence, though he has a powerful need for both. He will have to choose.

It wasn't clear to me at first what made his choice so painful. Certainly the Mercedes Man seemed to sit at the heart of Jack's self-image. He made that little house and full-time staff sound so good, I wondered why I'd never thought of it. But what about his attachment to Jane?

Jack insisted on his love for her, but he repeatedly undid those loving statements with small carps. Jane was not as devoted a sailor as he, always got sunburned and made him turn back. She has two ill-trained dogs who ruin her carpets and he was damned if he would put up with that. Jack always seemed to be looking around the room for someone better, and that initially made me skeptical about the depth of his feeling.

I was wrong. I learned that in one session when Jack unexpectedly brought Jane in to meet me. The content of the session was unremarkable but their interplay told it all. As Jane spoke, Jack listened carefully, curving his arm around the top of the couch toward her. She talked to me, but Jack looked toward Jane and every edge in him blurred. I don't see love that often, especially not in my office, and probably you don't see it that frequently either. But we do not doubt it when we see it. Jack looked at her steadily, with complete tenderness and connection.

Oh, I thought. Oh. That's the way it is. He loves her. That is the truth he can't get comfortable with. I wonder why.

Strong attachment is clearly an awkward fit for Jack. He wriggles around, pushing Jane away, sleeping at her apartment but leaving absurdly early the next morning, lunching defiantly with former girlfriends currently labeled "just friends." Jack seems driven to leave a little room for some other, newer, more elusive person. I don't know why, and Jack doesn't either. But he has a theory.

Jack has a lifetime history of sexual infidelity, no matter which woman is his primary partner. Perhaps, he speculates, after these six years together, Jane is more of a beloved sister than a romantic partner. Wouldn't it be impossible for him to be happy in a marriage with only familiar, comfortable sex?

I drew a cartoon sketch of Jack's penis holding a gun to his head, forcing him into a black car, with a stick figure of Jane left behind at the corner. That about summed up Jack's theory.

When Jane did discover that Jack was having an affair, her composure cracked completely. She was unable to get out of bed; she was weeping in restaurants. Her anger and pain made Jack furious. Jack recognized that his fury was irrational, but he felt it nonetheless. He was outraged that Jane caught him by looking over his cell phone bill. He was livid when Jane confronted him publicly at a happy hour they both frequent, blaming her for unnecessarily embarrassing them both. Jack's anger with Jane was no surprise. Anger, after all, is a time-honored balm for guilt.

Blaming Jane was not Jack's only distraction from his conflict. He also simply avoided his problem as much as possible. He didn't think about marriage unless Jane wiggled her ring finger in his face. He denied that the new flirtation, which he was conducting by phone and long lunch, was a potential threat. ("I'm not sleeping with her," he protested to me when I suggested that he was beginning an affair, as though an affair begins with penetration and not one instant before.)

Like everyone uncertain of marriage, Jack resented Jane for every imperfection that might make the decision to marry her more difficult. ("I can't get her to spend money on herself," he once complained. "Jeez," I attempted to sympathize, "that sounds like a hell of a problem.") Jane has flaws, of course—she's irritatingly social, definitely possessive, watches far too much television, doesn't do her share of the cleaning up. His life would be cluttered by these and other negative features if he got closer and lived with her. Why should he? Well, because he'll lose her if he doesn't. But will he lose himself if he does?

ACTION: Blaming Jane, fantasizing about having it all, denying flirtations even to himself, and playing for time are all dodges from Jack's difficult choice. While he dodged, the relationship got worse. Jack knew he had to take some productive action—that's why he hired a therapist.

Psychotherapy is not always a cattle prod, but Jack conceived of it that way. My job, as Jack construed it, was your basic psychotherapist-as-border-collie. He would raise an issue, drop a hint, signal a troubling feeling, and I would return to it again and again, while he feinted and darted around it. I went along, clarifying that our goal was for him eventually to become the shepherd, nipping at the heels of his own roaming impulses, fantasies, and rationalizations so he could head more directly toward whatever goal he chose.

We began with blame. The medicine for blame is interruption and empathy. Every time Jack held some flaw of Jane's accountable for his conflict, I asked him to explain the problem from her point of view.

"She calls me three times a night when I'm home for the evening."

"What do you think she's worried about?"

"Whether I'm home alone or calling other women."

"Are you calling other women?"

"Sometimes."

So we are back to Jack. Jack's dilemma was created by two conflicting needs in him, not by some flaw or failure of Jane's. His eventual attention shift from outer to inner was a very big first step. Or maybe he just got tired of the empathy exercise.

Jack broke through his own denial by being willing to discuss his flirtations so he could make conscious sexual decisions instead of morning-after sexual apologies. He said becoming self-aware was pretty much ruining his fun.

Finally, we closely inspected Jack's fantasy that if he met "the right woman," his own struggle between independence and attachment would disappear. Jack imagined that the right woman would exert such continuous sexual allure that he would never have to struggle against his own unfaithful impulse.

That fantasy—that another person will resolve all your conflicts about commitment and freedom—is a very powerful cultural wizard. This part of Jack's psychotherapy was a look behind the curtain. If you have the courage to look, the wizard shrinks down to size. Both Dorothy in Oz and Jack in my office had to make the time-honored discovery that they have the power to get *themselves* home, once they decide that home is where they want to be.

Jack, confronting his difficult choice head-on, is facing what hurts. The next step is to develop a vision of what might feel better.

Create a Vision

None of us deliberately leaves a comfort zone unless we can picture ending up someplace better. For Jack, developing a clear, positive vision presented his most difficult obstacle. He began therapy because he couldn't see himself happy without Jane, and he couldn't envision himself comfortably forsaking all others either. Where could he go from there?

Toward the end of our first six months together, Jack did report a focusing moment. He watched Jane on the beach one afternoon, making a towel tent so a friend's five-year-old could change out of her swimsuit in privacy. Jane looked so natural, so loving in the role, that Jack flashed on the thought "Coming home to a family with Jane wouldn't be so bad."

Jack instantly backed away from this thought. He and Jane fought that night, over sex and his flirtations, and he certainly did not share his vision of a future with her. But the flashing picture of coming home to Jane, of Jane being his home, had insinuated itself in a new way. If he lets go of his Mercedes, there could be *another* comfort zone out there.

ACTION: One day I asked Jack why the Man in the Black Mercedes couldn't become the Couple in the Black Mercedes? He turned that over and over, tossing it out, then returning to it. He began to refine it himself, changing it from my version to his own. We talked about Scott and Zelda, about whom neither of us knows much, so we were free to fabricate an image to suit Jack's need. We talked about other cool couples—Warren and Annette, Paul and Linda. (I almost wrecked the whole thing with Bill and Melinda Gates. I had to remind myself to let Jack generate his own icons.)

Jack returned to that couples image several times, once reminding me of the lyrics to "Moon River":

> "Two drifters, off to see the world.
> There's such a lot of world to see . . ."

There is a glamour in the lyric that he liked. Maybe he won't need to let go of his vision of the Man in the Black Mercedes. Maybe he'll only have to enlarge it.

Make a Decision

Jack is aware of so many differences between himself and Jane. How should he decide if this is the woman with whom to make such an emotional leap? How will he know when his happy bachelor horse is dead?

First, like most of us, Jack made one of those pros and cons lists, revealing his touching hope that relationships can be cost-accounted. A sample from Jack's list: "Pro: She is completely loyal. Con: She can't keep up with me on bike trips and other women can."

It is early in our work together. I try to do something productive with his list.

Me: "So you're telling me she slows you down."

Jack: "Right. I guess so."

Me: "Where is it you are trying to go in such a hurry?"

Jack: "I hate it when you get psychological."

We return to new items on the list, until eventually the list dies of its own dead weight.

List abandoned, there are two things to do to facilitate big decisions. Jack did both of them. He scrutinized himself to discover if he had some intuitive sense of direction. With that guidance, he risked a series of small, critical decisions to move himself forward.

ACTION: Jack developed a personal method of examining his shifting value system. Instead of talking directly about himself, he examined his reactions to his male friends, their feelings about Jane, and their own relationships with women. These friends served as a projection screen where Jack could evaluate his own feelings from a safe distance.

Jack's buddies liked Jane, even appeared to root for her. But Jack always reported an undercurrent of jocular warning, a constant "watch out, she's gonna getcha" that matched Jack's defensive posture in the relationship. Then a close friend survived a ruthless divorce and, amazing to Jack, quickly remarried. "There are too few good women," the friend said. "When you find one, close the deal." By contrast, when Jack began a romantic fling with a much younger woman, one or two friends smiled and called him an asshole to his face.

Somewhere along the line, the values in this friendship group, in Jack's perception of the group, or in Jack himself, shifted. They have made the full pendulum swing from Woody Allen to Alan Alda—that is, from hot lust overlooking Central Park to long-term love in New Jersey.

Intuitive direction usually only puts you partway down the path. Jack still has to make a decision. Jane wants marriage. Should he leave his comfort zone and marry her? Could he be faithful, even if he "decided" to be? Jack has serious doubts; there are just too many women, all around. I suggested he regard commitment like his earlier decision to quit smoking. It doesn't matter how badly you may sometimes want a cigarette. You have successfully quit if you don't put one in your mouth.

Jack needed some sort of trial period where he could test himself and his own willpower. I recommended that he try for a *fresh start*, a technique of labeling some period of time as the end of one era and the potential beginning of another. Jack was a real estate developer and a former associate invited him into a partnership developing a resort hotel in St. Croix, which would require a three-month stay on the island. He was drawn to the business opportunity. I strongly encouraged him to view it as a psychological opportunity as well. A three-month break could be his opportunity to test his capacity for commitment, one cigarette at a time.

Properly tried, this three-month break was an ideal chance to get off Jack's traffic circle. Three months out of town would free him of the shadowy half romances that were clouding his relationship with Jane. He would have a clean slate where every choice would, in effect, indicate a decision. Either Jack would avoid competing relationships or he would choose to have one while he was away. Either way, he would be answering his commitment question and establishing a direction for his future.

In order for this fresh start to guarantee progress, Jane had to be party to the plan. Jack agreed to take that step. He left for St. Croix with the stated understanding that he and Jane were still closely connected, but he had made no promises about the future. He was no longer denying the consequences of infidelity, however, nor blaming his uncertainty on Jane's shortcomings. When he left, Jack was able to state his emotional agenda to me very clearly.

"I don't know what will happen with Jane and me, and I don't know what I want to have happen. But I do know that if I get involved with any other woman while I'm there, I will tell Jane the truth, because it will mean that I've made a decision about us and she has a right to know."

Jack seemed freer to contemplate commitment now that he was far away. When he did, he started asking deeper questions, inviting us to wonder what made him shy away from commitment in the first place. When we first met, in Jack's mind a man who escaped a woman's clutches was triumphant on the face of it. Now he looked more deeply.

Identify Your Pattern
What will be lost if Jack abandons his Mercedes Man image? Is it youth, is it freedom, is it sexual conquest, is it just the entrenched comforts of twenty years of old familiar choices? Over our time

together, the image that resonated most strongly with Jack was the painful idea of closing a door.

We begin to talk about Jack as always being most comfortable having one foot out the door—always with a mate, but looking over her shoulder; always in a business, but open to others; settled into a house, but never thinking of it as a permanent home. It's certainly a great attitude for breadth of experience, but it makes depth of experience an unlikely possibility.

Any number of factors might have pushed Jack in this direction. For one thing, Jack is a charismatic extrovert who would make a friend at a bus stop if he had three minutes to kill. Even my doorman once remarked on what a great guy he seemed to be. Jack's charming interpersonal ease surely created many more opportunities with women than most men ever experience.

Too, Jack has been in training as a ladies' man since childhood. He's a third-born and only son, doted on by sisters, mother, and aunts, and so is comfortable with and interested in women in return. It all adds up to a whole lotta lovin' of and by Jack.

At the same time, he and Dad consciously cultivated his "man's man" identity—biking harder, hunting together, and priding themselves on never touching a dirty dish. Jack's man's man is desired by women, a conqueror of women, but is never possessed by a woman.

I get it now. The Man in the Black Mercedes is the Lone Ranger updated as a real estate developer. Wasn't the Lone Ranger always leaving town when the job was done?

Becoming conscious of a life pattern can be a very empowering thing. You can take a look at where it works for you and you can get a sense of how it gets in your way. Jack's native charm, his birth order, his unique relationship with Dad, his special family position have all probably contributed to his urgent push toward the new and different and more and better. Jack had always been clear about how his sense of freedom worked for him. Now, with respect to Jane, he could see how his old pattern might be getting in his way.

A useful theme was developing. Jack began to see closing a door as an act of courage that had been out of his range. Closed doors made him anxious; therefore closed doors became something to aspire to. Of course, "aspiring to" doesn't put you all the way there. To close a door meant Jack had to deal with a loss.

Let Go

If Jack closed his romantic door and married Jane, he would be letting go of more than sexual opportunity. Jack would be letting go of a cherished image of himself. That potential loss seemed to hurt as much as anything else.

Jack dreaded that loss. "I went to my buddy's this weekend and played with his kids for a good hour. It was fun. Maybe I'd want kids someday. I don't see why not. But after that hour I was done. Totally done. My friend has to be completely on duty. He doesn't even get high anymore." Pause. "I don't get high much anymore either. But I know I could."

"It's important to you to know you're free to do whatever you used to do, whether you want to do it or not," I suggest.

He smiles. "I don't want to give up like everybody else," he says.

"Like who?"

If he let go of his special identity, would he be letting down his dad? Was he partly living out his freedom for the dad who wished on Jack opportunities with women that he himself didn't have? Yes, probably partly.

By refusing to settle down, was he remaining loyal to his mom and his sisters, never replacing his first allegiance to them with a permanent female partner of his choice? Yes, probably partly.

Jack believes that his mom and dad, his sisters, even his friends have been invested in his wild-bird status, and that has encouraged him to overvalue it. I ask Jack to consider that perhaps they, too, may have grown and changed. Perhaps what they found important about his life ten or fifteen years ago is less appealing now. He is allowed to change, too, you know. We all are. He considers that.

Right around here Jack starts to be happier.

Face Your Fear

In his three months away, Jack worked fourteen-hour days on his new hotel, avoiding other women much as he had in his early days with Jane. His mental image of the phone call to Jane, telling her that he had started to date, acted as his strongest deterrent.

Occasionally, in our weekly phone sessions, Jack would report on a close call with some pride—an attractive sales rep whose invitation for a drink he turned down; an old Philadelphia fling who wanted to holiday with him for a week or so. To each he said no and pulled away. When I asked him why, he said, "It was just too much trouble." Or, "Been there. Seen that movie."

I thought these comments indicated that Jack had made his decision, albeit behind his own back. His return to Philadelphia, though, meant acknowledging that decision up front—a considerably more uncomfortable prospect.

With Jane's accusations and Jack's guilty anger out of the way, his fears showed up in sharp relief. They came down to one nightmare theme: What if I make a mistake?

What if he can't stand to live with Jane? What if he cheats on her and breaks her heart? What if she is the absolutely wrong woman and he is trapped because she is totally dependent on him? What if he meets his romantic ideal but he can't have her because he's stuck with Jane? What if he loses half his assets in a divorce?

Would this be what the talk shows call "fear of commitment"?

ACTION: How do you bring yourself to face a fear? First, *mentally separate what you want from what you fear*. Do this clearly, consciously, and do it over and over.

Jack is going to walk across these burning psychological coals for one reason: He is going toward something he desires. That something is Jane. It is love and an image of the two of them together in a safe harbor. He and I have been elaborating this vision of the Couple in the Black Mercedes for some time.

In one session I draw another little cartoon. He is a stick figure at the center of a circle, alone. Around him is that ring of anxious "what ifs." He can only get to what he wants by pushing through that ring. Or, he can avoid the ring and stay where he is, alone. Jack puts the cartoon in his wallet. It's a bad drawing but it's a powerful thought.

Next, we test strategies to reduce Jack's anxiety so his fears are tolerable. We use some cognitive techniques, listing his fears and then inverting them, providing substitute rational thoughts to reduce anxiety. "What if she's the wrong person?" becomes "What if she's my soul mate and I lose her because I'm chicken?" "What if I cheat?" becomes "I can decide how I will act with other women."

"What if I lose half my assets in a divorce?" became "What if I'm in a better financial position with her in my life than without her?" With this novel thought, Jack found himself thinking of the financial advantages of living together. Why did they need two mortgages, two lawns to mow, two sets of storm windows to put in? He wanted to simplify his life. Didn't she?

It turns out she didn't, at least not without being married. For some time it looked to me like this would be a deal breaker. Jane was totally against living together without marriage. Why would she give up her home without a clear commitment about her future?

Jack was totally against marriage without living together. He just felt too afraid. Why would he give up being the Man in the Black Mercedes without testing out his new vision? Uh-oh. Stuck again.

Jack retreated to blame, focusing in detail on all the potential difficulties of living with Jane. He withdrew, and brooded, but he did not begin an affair. Jane did nothing much, seemingly content to have a faithful Jack living in a separate house. At this point I suggested an intervention.

Jack had already taken the first two steps to face his fears. He had defined his fears as separate from his desires and he had done cognitive restructuring to reduce his anxiety. His third step would be to actively work against his fear.

Fear makes us passive. Activity makes us strong. Maybe it would be to Jack's benefit that it was not easy to get Jane to agree to living together. I suggested he work toward that goal. The work itself would be medicine for Jack's fear.

What could Jack do to make Jane more comfortable with the idea of living together? Eventually Jack stopped sulking and began actively seducing her toward his way of thinking. He showed how he would make room for her, insisted that she give due credit for all the ways he had changed out of love for her. He had made the leap of faith, he said. Now he wanted a similar vote of confidence in their relationship from her. In all the arguments

Jack was putting forth to persuade Jane, he was also easing his own anxiety.

I imagine it was his passion that convinced her. Jane put her house on the market and moved herself and her unruly dogs into Jack's larger home. They had a clear understanding that the arrangement should eventually lead to marriage, though no timetable was set. "If we're married" slid quietly, conversationally into "when we're married" and they earmarked the profits from the sale of Jane's house for a splendid honeymoon plus an addition they are thinking of building onto the house. Media room? Nursery? I'm definitely rooting for the latter.

Jack was no longer in therapy at the time of his wedding, so I don't know his feelings on that particular day. But I saw him a year later when he came in to discuss a business dilemma. He mentioned Jane frequently, sharing her point of view as well as his own. And he always included, with pride, her new title: "My wife says . . . ," "My wife believes . . ." Together they are a comfort zone.

Jack's story is unique, as yours will be when you resolve to escape your own comfort trap and move forward in your life. But, like Jack, if you find yourself stuck you will need to press yourself through the same seven steps to arrive on a new shore.

You will need to force yourself to face what hurts and to develop a clear and compelling vision of how your life might be better. You'll need to make a potentially difficult decision about whether the timing for change is right. You'll want to look back and understand how the pattern of your life has led you to this point and what that pattern might say about your next move. Then you'll have to let go of some rewards or relationships or beliefs or feelings that are holding you back. Finally, you will move forward to face the ring of anxiety that stands between you and what you want.

Each of these steps has its own obstacles, some of which you may encounter as you break through your own barriers. In the following chapters I'll take you step-by-step through the process, pointing out potential problems and outlining every successful strategy for circumventing those problems and keeping yourself on track.

This book is a road map. As with any map, you might be able to get where you're going without it, but it's so much more direct with one. Then again, without a map many of us just stay home. After all, it's so comfortable.

CHAPTER 3

FACE WHAT HURTS

You may not know exactly where you're going in life, but you know if you're not getting there. How do you know? Simple. You feel it.

Not getting where you want to go comes in a dozen emotional flavors but all of them are sour. You feel anything from fury to frustration, from guilt to grief. Or your life is entirely without flavor—flat, hollow. Each of these is the experience of pain and each is sending you a signal. Whether that signal occurs in the presence of a very active and ongoing misery or the simple absence of fizz, its message should be clear: Something hurts. Face it.

Shoulda, woulda, coulda. Pain certainly should be a clear signal that some new action is required. But it hardly ever is. It is also an unwelcome signal, so we do what we can to block it before we listen to what it has to say. It's easier to distract ourselves from the pain—medicate it, ignore it, dream about how it will magically disappear, point the finger at its cause—than to endure the discomfort of changing what is familiar.

Change is an awkward, irritating, even tormenting process and no reasonable person flings herself cheerfully on this pyre. We come to it kicking and screaming, but first we don't come to it at all. Here's what we do instead: we *avoid*, *blame*, *deny*, and *fantasize*.

Avoidance, blame, denial, and fantasy are the emotional caves where we take refuge from our own pain. Most of us spend time wandering in and out of these havens, taking shelter from anxiety and from the effort required to overcome it. Some time in these caves is restorative. A lifetime in the cave is just dark.

Avoidance

How powerful, how persuasive, how epidemic is avoidance? Plain and simple, avoidance is the root of most of your misery. And mine.

Life presents problems; problems make us uncomfortable; avoidance reduces that discomfort, though only in part and only for a while. Still, "in part" and "for a while" can be powerful relief, however temporary.

Classic avoidance strategies involve sedation by alcohol, drugs, food, or television, any one of which is more powerful when combined with any other. So, for example, stoned in front of your TV with a bag of Doritos in one hand and a beer in the other is an almost unbeatable combination for avoiding the pain of facing what hurts. I have worked with people who spent a decade or so in just such an after-work-hours zombie state. Where, they wonder, did the time go?

Be clear. Those TV shows we wouldn't miss, those Krispy Kremes, wine with dinner, or even the occasional recreational drug, if we could tell the truth about it, can all be life enhancers. But each is so easy to abuse, so paralyzingly, life-cripplingly *comforting*, that most of us have to guard against toxic excess even if we begin by indulging only a little.

I've listed the avoidance classics, but the fact is almost anything done to excess can become a successful avoidance technique. For example, exercise, sex, work, and love are all life essentials. But I've had patients who became marathon runners to avoid being home and some who had frequent casual sex in order to guard against the risks of intimacy. I've worked with plenty of people whose time-consuming work helps them avoid the rigors of relationships and an equal number whose passionate quest for love was mostly in hope of avoiding work.

Sleep, golf, perfectionism, procrastination, or even obsessive lawn care can all be excellent avoidance strategies. When taken to the proper extremes, any and all of these methods will temporarily ease emotional pain, making it possible for you to stay in your familiar comfort zone.

One less obvious but highly popular avoidance technique is worth noting, namely the chronic complaint. The complainer reduces discomfort by venting about a problem instead of facing the anxiety of fixing it. You know this well if you have ever been held hostage on the phone by a complaining friend:

The abusive client has made yet another outrageous demand—would you believe anybody could make you deliver work on the way to the airport for your vacation? (But your friend is on her way to the client, never saying no, never setting limits.)

The married lover broke yet another promise—would you

believe she went on a trip with the very husband she says she hasn't slept with in months? (But your friend is back at the bar next week, admiring his lover's tan and listening to her excuses.)

The selfish brother made yet another self-absorbed choice—would you believe he forgot to walk the dog, though it was the one thing asked of him in exchange for years of caretaking and personal favors? (But your friend is over at her brother's again next Saturday, cleaning up his place because he needs help.)

Food, drugs, alcohol, and television numb you to the painful parts of your comfort zone; complaining takes the energizing sting out of that pain. Or you may have some other rabbit hole to disappear down, giving you instant relief from your anxiety. But the price of that relief is high.

Avoidance often makes your initial problem worse. Lie to avoid a husband's displeasure and, if the lie is discovered, displeasure becomes outrage. Avoid confronting a friend who hurts your feelings and the friend repeats and repeats the offense. Postpone completing that master's degree and sudden downsizing may thrust you into the job market without it. Ignore the monthly breast self-exam and the tiny lump is no longer treatable.

Even when problems don't get worse, we do. Normal concerns may calcify into fears and phobias. What was only momentary discomfort driving over a bridge becomes an extra hour's commute because lately you've been avoiding the bridge altogether. An early childhood reluctance to be called on expands to silence you in business meetings, blocking your professional advancement. Avoiding problems causes problems of its own, and so we flounder, suffering, victims of our own tendency to avoid.

Too, avoidance is imperfect. We push our problems away, but they push back, waking us to white nights, leeching into back pain, threading a thin agitation through the layers of our days.

Problems we are avoiding find us symbolically, making us squirm with dim self-recognition in movies like *American Beauty*, novels like *The Corrections*, paintings like De Chirico's. We turn away from these signals, too, seeking escapist movies, happy endings, romantic plots, decorative art, and the perfectly loyal circle of *Friends.*

Still, problems creep in through the cracks, in dreams, in absentminded mental drifting. You are driving cheerfully out of your garage when you begin a mental rant: *The damned neighbor left her garbage can where my flowers are planted again. Why is she such a pig? She has no right to do that. I should call her up and tell her flat out that she is over the property line, so back off.*

You have intended to call her for the last two months. You just haven't managed to make the call.

Would the call change things? Of course. For one thing, she might move the garbage can. You and she might see the problem differently and negotiate some middle-ground solution together. At the very least, you will have taken the problem out of your head, where there is no possibility of solution, and brought it into the real world, where something might change.

But you avoid the phone call, because it's uncomfortable. There's that electric fence of anxiety, no longer an abstract concept but a real sense of agitation, making itself known, perhaps, in a stomach flutter as you approach the phone.

What is that dread all about? Well, nothing rational, you will be quick to point out. Your neighbor might be awful on the phone, though you admit it isn't all that likely. Even if your neighbor is unpleasant, so what? Why do confrontation, disapproval, rejection, or failure loom so menacingly that we avoid facing their possibility, even knowing all we stand to gain?

They hurt. It's as simple as that.

That dread, that instinctive avoidance of pain, seems a perfectly natural, profoundly human part of our nature. If something might cause pain, we avoid it. Deliberately challenging your comfort zone causes anxiety. Facing problems causes anxiety. Anxiety is painful. Avoid it!

But, avoid pain and you can't solve the problem; avoid pain and the problem may get worse; avoid pain and you'll be stuck on your dead horse forever.

So how do we get ourselves to face what hurts, when our natural tendency is to duck and cover? In a word: *Discipline*.

Developing Discipline

If your horse is dead, self-discipline is an essential, perhaps the quintessential weapon. Deliberately extending your comfort zone puts you in a fight against yourself. Discipline is what allows you to emerge the winner. It is the main source of spiritual muscle that will force you to face that fence of anxiety and eventually get you to the other side.

"Discipline" may be a hot-button word for you. Some read it as a synonym for "willpower," with its implication of weakness and indictment for past failures. ("If you want to lose weight, why don't you try a little discipline?") Others associate "discipline" with the imposition of outside authority raining "shoulds" on all your fun.

In truth, "discipline" has echos of both of these offensive meanings. But they are not the heart of the concept. At its core, discipline is a strategy for meeting your own requirements by creating the habit of letting your higher-order self take charge of your own impulsive brat—at least much of the time.

Peerless psychologist and philosopher Scott Peck eloquently defines discipline as "a system for dealing constructively with the pain of problem solving, instead of avoiding that pain." If you don't already have such a system in place, you can develop one. Without it, though, you may find yourself chained to the stale safety of a narrow comfort zone, like my patient Ryan.

Ryan, thirty-four, is one of Philadelphia's many uncertain sons who are swallowed into a family business after an unfocused cruise through college. Currently a salesman at his family's packaging company, Ryan is one of the heirs presumptive, though he is not business-school educated like his younger cousins. Ryan, however, has a street cunning developed in his earlier years of selling recreational drugs to friends. He has used these skills to carve out a comfortable niche as a packaging salesman, massaging relationships, icing over delivery failures with easy charm, and appreciating the occasional kickback that comes his way.

The niche is financially comfortable, but it's frustrating, too. Ryan wants to expand the family business into packaging and transportation for music tours and theatrical road shows. He wants his professional life to have some glamour, creativity, and contact with more interesting people. His grandfather, who still has the firm's ownership in his tight grip, ignores his ideas, complaining instead about Ryan's hours, his sales volume, his paperwork. There are confrontations in the office that extend to the Sunday dinner table when the family gathers at the grandparents'.

Ryan detests those dinners, his powerless position, and the everlasting parental oversight. Frankly, he's sick to death of boxes. Still, what else could he do? It's worth too much to walk away and leave it all to the cousins.

Ryan's wife sent him to see me, concerned about his renewed

pot smoking and probable depression. His complaints about his family were endless and she dreaded the mandatory Sunday suppers where the men argued while the women cleared the table. Ryan has tried to tune out the whole mess, but lately its volume has been increasing.

The day-to-day problems that stem from his halfhearted work ethic hurt Ryan; the resulting family criticism hurts Ryan; the tedium of his professional life hurts Ryan; the stifled ambition hurts Ryan. Ryan has avoided facing these problems, stuck in the comfortable role of family screw-up, procrastinating, resisting, complaining, getting high, and generally passively making his problems worse.

The hinge on which the closed door of Ryan's avoidance opens into problem solving is . . . discipline.

Ryan stewed during our early sessions, explaining what was frustrating about his work. "My grandfather is wowed by all that get there early, stay late bull, which I think is totally about control. I mean, I tell him, 'Who am I going to sell boxes to at eight o'clock in the morning?'"

"So that's what it would take to impress your grandfather," I say. "What would it take to impress you?"

"What do you mean?"

"What are you trying to accomplish at the office?"

"I sell boxes."

"What do you think about your box salesmanship?"

"I could do better."

"Oh?"

"Yeah, I could get through those bids that have been sitting in a pile on my carpet. I could maybe service some accounts a little more frequently. I know I'm supposed to do all this shit, and I'd probably sell a million more boxes. I'd probably feel better, too. Some mornings I swear I'm going to have at it, pretend I'm like my cousin Billy and dive into one of the piles. But I can't get myself to do it."

"Why not?"

"Because I hate selling boxes."

Here is my opening. I am about to make a sales pitch for self-discipline, that single best medication for avoidance. I do not expect Ryan to be buying my pitch, not at this point. But discipline is a muscle and if Ryan can be persuaded to work out regularly, he might harness his imagination and hustle into something productive for himself.

"I hate selling boxes," he repeats. I must have been quiet too long.

"Right. But so what?" I say. "If you've decided to do something, why not do it whether you hate it or not? Discipline, you know, it's acting according to what you think instead of how you feel at the moment. That's the only way any of us gets ourselves to do the hard stuff."

"But if I could get the family to make the business changes I'm thinking about, I wouldn't hate it so much. I'd want to get to work early. I'd want to make the sales calls. I just can't get through the stuff now because I'm sick of boxes."

Ryan's choices are predictably determined by his emotional cycle. Guilt and obligation press him toward a task, resistance and discomfort repel him from it. In the absence of outside pressure, like most of us, Ryan has great difficulty confronting something unpleasant on his own. Professional deadlines sometimes add their weight to the equation, forcing him to complete a task despite his own discomfort. Then he's apt to report that it wasn't so bad, didn't take as long as he had feared. Still, the next time he is confronted with an unpleasant task, or a complex life problem, he avoids it again.

Do you recognize yourself? To the degree that you do, avoidance is holding you back. Like Ryan, consciously practicing the following four simple principles of discipline will move you forward.

1. Do the Hard Stuff First

Certainly delayed gratification is the heart of middle-class morality, taught to our children when they toddle (First the peas, or no dessert, Ryan!). We extend it through middle school to students who are working toward college and carry its core concepts into our workplace (First the cold calls, then the coffee break, Ryan!) and our homes (First help me with the dishes, then playoff game, Ryan!).

In the areas of your life where you routinely delay gratification and do the hard stuff first, you are probably functioning fairly smoothly, with a low degree of emotional struggle. You are gritting your teeth and doing the work, or the workout, making the phone call or facing the friend and then—task complete, pain endured, and maybe even mission accomplished—you are rewarded.

None of us functions evenly in all areas of life. You know what your comfort zone is. It probably includes some habitual delay of gratification, some problems confronted routinely and resolved as a matter of course. Others are habitually avoided.

Why? Typically those problems we avoid move us closer to the edge of our comfort zone, and out there the anxiety is high.

Ryan, for example, chafes against the restrictions of an adult identity, and the paperwork he shirks is his own little self-destructive pocket of resistance. Of course his evasion tactics backfire. The higher the pile of undone chores, the more psychologically menacing that pile becomes. He carries his untended obligations everywhere, feeling frustrated and burdened.

2. Do What You Think, Instead of What You Feel

Discipline is a cognitive function. It involves decision making, planning, and rational judgment. Certainly behaviors flow from it, and acts of discipline evoke feelings—power, dread, reluctance, pride, smugness. But fundamentally, discipline means behaving according to what you have decided is best, regardless of how you feel at the moment.

Most of our natural maturation moves in the direction of discipline. Over time, and with effort, we behave increasingly as a result of our own judgment and control and less and less at the mercy of our own emotional states. A baby is entirely emotion. A wise adult knows what he or she feels, but then acts according to how he or she thinks best. Sometimes those acts are perfectly in line with our feelings, and sometimes (as when you are biting your tongue with an ungrateful client or an oversensitive daughter-in-law) we do quite the opposite of what we feel, and then pat ourselves on the back for it.

Ryan is struggling against himself professionally. We know what his family wants, but Ryan himself has yet to commit to a professional vision. He is wallowing in his postadolescent comfort zone, avoiding decision making on his own behalf so he can only react emotionally to the decisions made for him. Rebellion is a beautiful thing, but when you overthrow the czar, you have to be prepared to govern. It's not enough for Ryan to resist authority. He has to become his own authority and take directions from himself. That's his stretch, that's where we're aiming.

3. Take Any Small Step in the Right Direction

Preparation to govern oneself comes in small steps. Certainly Ryan does not need a full-blown life plan in order to build self-discipline. Like all of us, he can practice with what's on the plate today.

There is one best way for Ryan to reduce the frustration of his immediate psychological clutter: Overcome his resistance and, as he says, "dive into the pile." But as good as his intentions sometimes are, there is a wall between himself and the task. That wall is a reluctant sense of agitation, a discomfort, an anxiety, and Ryan allows himself to be repelled by it almost every time.

The good news is, that wall of anxiety is tissue-thin. If Ryan approached his pile, started with the first piece of paper, allotted just a few minutes a day to the task, his anxious resistance would diminish enormously. If you merely dial the neighbor's number and begin the conversation, your problem is beginning to be solved. Schedule the doctor's appointment, tell the friend you need to talk, open the unpaid bills, take any first step in the right direction, and sometimes that tissue wall is permanently demolished. Taking that step, then continuing through the wall, are acts of discipline.

4. Coach Yourself

Opportunities to practice self-discipline arise automatically every day of your life. The courage to face what hurts, however, has to be summoned. Courage, that inner juice, usually doesn't just rise to the fore of its own impetus. You'll have to talk to yourself, encourage yourself, reassure yourself. You'll say things like, "Come on, Judith, get this call over with. You'll feel so much better when it's done. There's really nothing to be afraid of. Even if he gets mad, it'll be over in a few minutes. Remember why you decided to do this. Don't be a coward. Stop thinking about this and just dial."

Ryan talked himself to his pile. "Dude, Michael Jordan is all focus. Tiger Woods is total focus. You could do ten minutes of focus, even if you are focusing on bullshit. There is a certain amount of bullshit in every job. You gotta be able to eat the pile." This would not have been my script, but Ryan found it encouraging. Try one of these, or try some other script, *but deliberately keep the dialogue going in your head.* Self-talk calls up courage, reinforces commitment, and keeps you conscious of the problem you need to resolve.

Courage, commitment, and conscious awareness are mental allies; they create a mind-set that supports disciplined behavior. Disciplined behavior faces you toward what hurts and provides the fortitude and focus necessary to solve problems that stand in your way. Then things get better, you are through the land mines of anxiety and on to some newer, sweeter comfort zone of your own creation.

Got it?

- Conscious awareness of how and what you are avoiding,
- A commitment to act, and
- Deliberate, ongoing internal pep talks to remind you of who you want to be and who you can be

will all build and reinforce self-discipline.

The more disciplined you are, the stronger will be your determination to solve problems rather than hiding from them.

It is that self-discipline that drives you to work on your brilliant idea after the first flush of enthusiasm has passed, discipline that gets you to the gym even though you are still smoking and you wonder if you should bother, discipline that forces you to talk to the boss even though you're afraid to hear what he has to say.

We are all somewhere on the continuum of developing discipline, taking two steps toward making a civil call to the rude neighbor and one step back with a childish kick to the trash can. One additional element is likely to be the deciding factor in whether you go forward or only around in circles. To the four principles of discipline, you must add *structure*.

Committing to Structure

Abby, twenty-nine, is jogging through a city park, trying to outrun her impulse to call Mitchell and invite him over. Mitchell will certainly come and have sex with her, but he won't stay for more; he has never stayed for more and Abby has almost given up hoping that he ever will. She is trying to ignore that one-more-time, just-tonight, maybe-this-time voice in her head, though she has never successfully outshouted it for long. As Abby jogs, she comes to a garden posted with a small sign that reads "Please stay on the path." That helps.

Abby has framed the problem for all of us. How do we stay on the path, focused and disciplined, when the path is littered with nettles of anxiety and it is so easy to turn back to the shelter of that familiar comfort zone?

How do you stay on the diet when you are four weeks into a

plateau and your daughter's boyfriend dumped her and she's taking it out on you?

How do you keep up the job search when the last two interviewers seemed to think you were being overpaid now?

How do you work on the marriage when your spouse is content with the explanation that the problem in the marriage is you?

How do you plan for retirement when you don't have a single passion outside your work?

How do you steel yourself to let your kid make her own mistakes when she actually starts making them?

How do you, or Abby, resist just one more night with the bad boyfriend when you're lonely and fantasy seems better than nothing?

Whatever trap you are trying to avoid—the comfort of food, a stifling job, marital silence, a completed career, or parental control—how do you move through the setbacks to new ground instead of turning and fleeing to familiar comfort?

You need to structure your path. It's the only way.

Here is what all effective people know and many of the rest of us struggle against: *Success is not spontaneous. It's a vision, plus an intention, plus a plan, plus effort.* Here's the big picture:

- Discomfort points you in a new direction, challenging your current comfort zone.
- Avoidance blunts that discomfort and misdirects your energy.
- The discipline inherent in delayed gratification, conscious judgment, and small steps in the right

> direction refocuses your energy toward your own new goal.
> - Structure supports your intention to reach that goal by identifying when, where, what, and how you are going to take those next steps.

Structure is involved in every problem you choose to face and solve. It is, in effect, your plan, detailed enough so you can see yourself solving your problem in your mind's eye. Structure takes you from your decision to solve a problem to your vision of the solution.

Let's go back to the neighbor who leaves her garbage can on your flowers. (I just hate her.) You are conscious of the problem, certainly, because it's making you churn. And perhaps you've even gone beyond complaining to your friends about that neighbor and you've committed to solving the problem yourself. You're nervous, but you have decided to make the phone call.

Now, what will increase the likelihood that you will actually *do* what you've decided to do? Structure!

Structure means you choose a time and a place for your phone call, have a tentative script for what you will say, and you can picture yourself saying it. It's helpful to talk to yourself: "Be brave, Judith. You'll feel so much better when you've made this call, so do it!" Add to that the decision to call tonight at seven, right after dinner, and to open up the phone call by saying "We have a problem I want to discuss with you. You might not be aware of it, but you've been leaving your trash can on the edge of the driveway where I planted bulbs last year. It bothers me a lot. Would you be willing to put it over on the side, where nothing is planted? I'd really appreciate it."

In real life, chances are great that you won't get through your

script or that the response you get will be other than what you an-
ticipate. That's fine. The purpose of the script is that it makes the
call easier for you, which will make it more likely that you'll
make the call. That's problem solving instead of avoidance.

Abby needs structure to support her intention to get off the
dead horse that is her affair with Mitchell. What hurts her is the
letting go. She'll face that more easily if she has a plan for how to
handle a Mitchell moment (call a friend, sit in a movie, jog,
write in her journal, try Match.com, write herself a letter coaching
herself to resist the call).

In my experience, Abby will also need to have a script available for those nights when Mitchell calls and dangles a relationship in front of her because he's feeling lonely or looking to get
laid. (He'll call, I'm sure he'll call. Abby's kind of devotion is too
delicious to give up altogether.)

That script, like any script you might need in order to face
what's hurting you, need only be an informal paragraph. My patients and I write them all the time. What's important is to have a
clear idea of your first sentence or two, getting the hard issue out
on the table before anxiety shoves you back into your cave. In
this sense the script can be your map of that first small step in the
right direction.

If (says wounded Abby) and when (says me) Mitchell next
calls to suggest that she come over for "Chinese food and a
movie," I recommended a bold script: "Thanks anyway, Mitchell.
Look, I don't want to hurt your feelings, but I think you need to
stop calling. Please don't feel bad. You've been a very pleasant
lover, and we had some fun times, but it's time for me to move
on. I'm sure you understand." As of our last session, Abby found
this script breathtakingly extreme and could only hope that she
could get out the words "Thanks anyway." Mostly she fantasizes

that Mitchell will never call again, and mournful though that will be, it will not be as hard as actually resisting his bait.

Jack found a short script helpful when he met with Jane before he left for St. Croix. "Jane, I love you, but I don't know if I'm capable of real commitment. I think I want this to work between us, but I know myself, too. I recognize that all these gray areas and half-flirtations are torturing both of us. I want to start with a clean slate in St. Croix and I promise you one thing: If I decide to have a date there, or be sexually involved with any other woman, I will tell you the truth about it. Then you can decide from there what you want to do. Can you live with that?"

Ryan could use a script when and if he had a professional presentation to make to his family. You might want to write down the first two sentences you will use when you approach your boss for the flextime schedule you daydream about, or to confront the friend who demeans you without seeming to know it. You just need a few sentences that put your difficult issue out in the open so your urge to avoid will be undercut. Then add to those sentences a mental time and place for delivery and you will have a support structure to face what hurts.

> Structure—what do I need to do, and then
>> when will I do it,
>> where will I do it,
>> what exactly will I say, do, ask—

will set you in motion when you've run aground. Structure allows you to execute the plan your judgment and courage have envisioned. Together, these tools and attitudes strengthen the self-discipline you'll need to face what hurts.

Remember, what you desire is on the other side of that wall of anxiety. *Self-discipline is the will to get over that wall; structure is the ladder.*

As we've noted, avoidance comes in many disguises: from habitual procrastination over your long to-do list to some delightful hobby that develops into an unproductive obsession. Whichever avoidance strategy you tend to use, discipline and structure will help you to face and resolve the problems that have frightened you into staying put.

Three avoidance strategies, though, are tenacious enough to be worthy of special note. They are habits of the mind so reasonable and effective at reducing anxiety that all of us use them unproductively from time to time. These three are blame, denial, and fantasy—dragons guarding the gates of your comfort zone.

Blame

Blame—which focuses on the question "Whose fault is it that I got stuck here?"—is essentially a brilliant delaying tactic. It funnels painful feelings away from yourself, all the while postponing your need to face the anxiety of leaving a comfort zone. Blame is psychological junk food—deliciously gratifying, harmless in small doses, lethal as a regular diet.

When focused on others, say, inadequate parents, insensitive bosses, selfish spouses, competitive friends, unjust social conditions, and the like, blame evokes the satisfaction of righteous indignation. Righteous indignation is then so fulfilling that some of us linger in the cul-de-sac of blame for years, successfully avoiding the anxiety of moving forward under our own steam. You will recognize this stuck person as the familiar quivering victim, always done to by someone and rarely able to acknowledge being the occasional doer.

In truth, we have all been done to by someone, and some of us unfairly wounded far worse than others. We are all victims on occasion and much of the pain in our lives is caused by someone else's cruelty or stupidity. Anger in those circumstances is just and healthy.

That line between clean anger and festering blame can be murky:

When Amy learns that her ex-husband is traveling in Vietnam and she says, "Where are the Viet Cong when you need them?" is she stuck flogging the old dead horse of a long-finished marriage or merely taking a momentary potshot at a tried-and-true adversary?

When Keisha rages that she didn't get pregnant because her infertility doctor wouldn't do inseminations on a Sunday, is her blame an accurate assessment of her medical care or a way to distract herself from the disappointing parenting choices ahead?

Paul has been tolerating two pleasant, incompetent employees who should have been fired long ago. He blames the supervisor who pressured him into hiring them, though he is the one who will have to do the firing. Is he accurately assessing office politics or just trying to evade a dreaded confrontation?

Laney's grandfather knocked her grandmother around, yet Grandmom stayed married; her father permitted her mother no outside friendships, yet Ma stayed married, too. How, she asks, can she be expected to leave her own disrespectful husband with role models like that? Is that blame or a simple statement of psychological fact?

In every case, of course, the answer is a little bit of both. Other people harm us and the stinging injury makes us howl. Anger pointing a finger is blame. That blame may be an accurate assessment of the cause of the injury. Whether it is or not, it can also be an effective avoidance technique. Two payoffs for the price of one thought. Plus, righteous indignation feels good. Who wouldn't linger here for a while?

Blame's magic is that it does not rely on a rational assessment of any situation. If you are given to blaming, you will be able to identify the person who hurt you, without any need to account for that person's motivation or point of view. (As you'll see in the empathy exercise, once you start seeing things from both your side and the other side, wholehearted blaming becomes more and more difficult.)

Sometimes blame is an arrow aimed squarely at one's own heart as a counterweight to the self-destructive impulses we allow to enslave us. *Hey, I know I shouldn't do this. I'm doing it anyway, but at least I'm willing to hate myself for it.* This mantra of self-criticism permits us an enormous amount of excess and transgression, although it seriously cuts into the fun that excess can be. Self-blame may become its own familiar comfort zone, allowing forbidden satisfactions and evoking the security that no one else can sneak up and criticize you because you are already harder on yourself.

Some situations lend themselves to blame. Enron employees know precisely at whom to point the finger when they face their financially rocky retirements. Unfaithful mates inflict so much pain that their unhappy spouses may be unable to see past that blame to a fruitful path for their own new lives.

But even without obvious evidence, any of us can find our way to blame if we are hurting. Jack, you remember, blamed Jane's tactics so as to avoid the truth of her accusations. Ryan blames his grandfather's controlling personality for the obstacles in his own professional path. He's right about his grandfather's personality. It definitely gets in his way. But Ryan gets in his own way more.

Rethinking What You Think: Eliminating Blame

There are really three effective strategies for getting beyond blame: rational responsibility, interruption and focus on future opportunities, and the magic bullet, empathy. I warn you, though, while each of these strategies will work, they require discipline and structure to succeed. There is something gluey about blame. It sticks easily where we first stash it, even if it's an inappropriate place. Only determined scraping removes it.

Rational Responsibility

Self-blame and its first cousin, guilt, are each a step to the extreme of a rational sense of responsibility. Holding yourself responsible for your actions is obviously necessary to challenging your comfort zone. But a sense of responsibility has reasonable boundaries. It is defined by an appropriate recognition of what you can and cannot control. Generally speaking, a sense of responsibility means that you see your part in some greater whole. You may not like it, you may not be proud of it, and you may not choose to repeat it the next time. But you recognize it and accept it for what it is.

Abby, for example, cycled from blame to guilt and back when we first began discussing her heartbreaking attachment to Mitchell. One week she was all self-loathing, contemptuous of her own "pathetic neediness." The next week or even the next minute she might be rocked by a gust of rage, blaming Mitchell for all the promises he dangled for no better reason than it was fun to see her rise to the bait. Both these emotional extremes are understandable, even natural, but neither would help Abby disconnect from Mitchell and move on. Only gaining a balanced perspective on her own issues and Mitchell's could help her tolerate the sharp blade of loss that accompanies letting go.

Self-blame and guilt are the histrionic exaggeration of that sense of responsibility. They are all feeling and hand-wringing, remorse and regret. Self-blame and guilt encourage overstatements. "It's all my fault" is usually as inaccurate a statement as "It's not *my* fault."

Responsibility is a rational assessment and that makes it a productive state of mind. It helps you see your way out of a comfort zone, in part because it reinforces your sense of having power and control. Guilt does the opposite, skewering you in place with an emotional tidal wave of self-hatred. The subtext of guilt is "I can never change. I'm just a bad person."

Self-blame and blaming others are opposite dodges, though certainly the same person can make use of both extremes. Generally, though,

- Blamers need to take a look at their own actions and maybe even apply a medicinal tincture of self-chastising guilt, while
- Self-blamers need to look up from that absorbing self-loathing and focus on future choices.

Interruption and Future Focus

When you're thinking something self-defeating, basically what you have to do is just stop thinking it. Yes, yes. I know that's easier said. But it definitely can be done. The quickest way to stop thought is to interrupt it—for example, catch yourself in the act of blaming and cut yourself short. Then replace the blame thought with a plan for improvement, a sense of hopeful possibility, or even a decision to make amends. Focusing on what you can do is so much more productive than regretting what you did or stewing over what was done to you.

Interruption is something with which a therapist or a friend you've enlisted can be helpful. For example, Ruth, who fled the world of dating she had spent months readying herself to enter, was caught up in self-loathing for her flight. In our early sessions she needed tremendous urging before she moved past her regret at missed chances and focused on dating opportunities yet to come. Ruth wanted to spend a lot of our time talking about her history of weakness and fear. She had theories about what made her so sensitive to rejection and, if left to her own self-critical bent, she would examine and castigate herself for every failure of nerve she could recall.

I think of this destructive self-analysis as building a case against yourself. Except in those rare instances when something positive can come of it, I try to interrupt it as early and as often as possible and recommend you do the same. Right now, what Ruth has is theories about what's wrong with her. I'd rather she had a date she enjoyed, and I don't see how the theories are going to get her there.

Even Ryan has a streak of self-recrimination—for example, regretting his pot smoking after a wasted weekend. I point out that it is so much easier to hate yourself in the morning than to stand against a self-destructive urge the night before. Some regret is galvanizing. Like Ryan, you'll know when you've hit the productive kind of regret if it comes with a structured plan for how you are going to handle things differently next weekend. Monday-morning regret that translates into structured support for reducing marijuana use and diving into the pile is emotional fuel for change. Without that structure, it's just whining.

Interruption, rational evaluation of responsibility, and a focus on future choices are good strategies for getting beyond blame so you can face what hurts. There is one other life skill that is absolute pesticide for the hardy weed of blame. Spray blame with a strong dose of empathy and it will wither.

Thinking What They Think: Empathy

Empathy: feeling what someone else feels, seeing the problem from another's point of view, standing in someone else's shoes. Now, empathy squared, or what I sometimes describe to my patients as a graduate course in empathy:

- Feeling what someone else feels, *even though that person hurt you*
- Seeing the problem from another's point of view, *even though you are certain that other point of view is wrong*
- Standing in someone else's shoes, *even though those shoes are currently walking all over you*

This should give you a sense of just how tough the empathy exercise is. Blaming is a kind of astigmatism that prevents the blamer from seeing his own role clearly. My job, then, is to help correct those distortions, to help you see your part in an event that hurt you. You play a role in what happens to you, most (though not all) of the time. Since that is the part you can change, let's take a look at it.

This is an unbelievably tricky business. To help anyone see his or her part in a painful event pretty much means asking him to see things from the point of view of the person he is blaming. In theory, this is empowering. In real life, this is infuriating.

When Ryan tells me what a jerk his grandfather was this week, the last thing he wants to hear is how he might have contributed to their little family dance by being a jerk himself. Still, seeing that truth could help him be less of his grandfather's victim and more of a contributor to the professional problem. He will have to bear down and be willing to see it. I will have to find a way to show it to him that does not make him hate me too much. I do not always succeed.

I introduce the idea of empathy, talk about how seeing a problem from your adversary's point of view may make you feel less of a victim, more of an equal opponent.

We practice over and over the basic empathy exercise: Empathy asks, What is the other person's point of view? What does it feel like to the other person? What are his or her interests? Where do they conflict with yours? Did this person do something intentionally against you, or did he or she act *for* him- or herself?

Hint: It always *feels* as if it was against you because, after all, it hurt you. But hurting you was not necessarily the motivation.

True enough, Ryan's grandfather is an old fart who resists change. But what in Ryan's behavior might make his suggested changes more threatening? (For example, Ryan's defiance of the traditional work hours isn't exactly a confidence builder.) True enough, Ryan is from a highly critical family that competes with one another more passionately than it cooperates. (But Ryan's college drug career has not enhanced their willingness to cooperate with him. Nor does his current pot use help build their respect.)

Sometimes I use the inimitable James Carville's language: "You think what you think. You have to think what they think." Ryan relates better to Carville than to a squishy idea like "empathy." Use whichever perspective fits you best, but do the empathy exercise. If it works, it will rouse you from the blame cave.

Seeing anything from the point of view of someone who has hurt you is pretty high-level stuff, intellectually and emotionally speaking. Ryan is smart and becomes gradually more psychologically minded as we work together. He doesn't crumple at the first new sight of his own responsibility. There is usually a cringe, of course, at something new he hadn't seen. But a cringe creates only momentary hesitation. Ryan can move past it.

A word of warning: Empathy means that you are open to another point of view, but not so open that your brains fall out. Frances might be empathetic to her alcoholic lover, recognizing that he would never be so vilely abusive were he not drunk, nor would he be drunk so often if he were not in the grip of a monstrous addiction. She might even empathize with the pain for which he is medicating himself with alcohol—the professional disappointments, family losses, and early injuries that occasioned his love affair with alcohol in the first place.

But none of this empathy should add up to her staying in the relationship. Empathy can help Frances stop blaming her lover for her unhappiness and take a hard look at her own fears.

Empathy should not be confused with a rationalization for tolerating abuse or misery. It's a tool for getting past blame so you can find your own way out.

Denial and Fantasy

Here's an elementary way to avoid facing what hurts: Simply put painful truths out of your conscious mind.

"I'm in denial," Lydia joked when I asked her what birthday she was celebrating on Saturday. She meant, "Every birthday reduces the chance that I will have a child and I handle that by ignoring the birthday."

Lydia, thirty-eight, has been in human resources at a large pharmaceutical company for eleven years and refers to herself as a "lifer." Her work itself is uninspiring but there's plenty of it, so she often feels burdened though never excited. Lydia is both thin and thin-skinned, easily hurt by the smallest slight, often angered by the insensitivity of others. She was drawn to human resources because she imagined it was a way to "carry the flag for humanity in the corporate world." She has, however, long since determined that her do-good impulses would be forever hampered by corporate policy and corporate lawyers. Now Lydia sees herself as merely a paper pusher.

When the corporation offers "exit packages" to pare its workforce, Lydia fantasizes that one will be dangled at her level. Then, she says, she'd take it and find more interesting work. But she never actively looks outside at what else might be possible for her. Lifers don't.

Besides, work for Lydia is merely the way she earns a living. In her barely whispered private identity, Lydia is a fabric artist, a quilter and weaver whose most satisfying hours are spent at her loom. She is wiry and nervous, happiest alone when she can smoke and weave and dream and feel safe. She longs to be part of the creative community, but she is still too hesitant to try her work at local galleries.

In her mind's eye Lydia sees herself in a messy house in Bucks County making art, surrounded by dogs and children. She wants children, but by ignoring her birthdays, she denies the limitations of her biological clock. Assisted by the occasional media celebration of a forty-five-year-old mother of twins, Lydia vaguely believes that she will have children "someday" when she meets the right guy. This guy would presumably favor country living, put Lydia in a pumpkin carriage, and plant her in a happy country home. Denial and fantasy—a suite of caves shelters Lydia from the discomfort of her loneliness and childlessness. As temporary shelter they make her life tolerable, but they also make her completely passive. Babies don't always come to she who waits.

In one session, Lydia described herself as one of those shivering women you see huddled outside the office building, standing in a coat in the small smoking area, holding a romance novel in one hand and a cigarette in the other. She can't seem to get herself in from the cold. Denial is the door she slams in her own face, trapping her in this lonely comfort zone. It keeps her from facing what hurts.

"There are none so blind as those who will not see" defines denial. Denial helps us tolerate difficult situations because we simply fail to recognize them—for example, when we fail to recognize the limitations of our aging joints, the unlikelihood of our recovery from an illness, or the warning signs of a mate's infidelity or a child's troubled adolescence.

Denial is the defense that is operating:

- When you don't feel worried about your company's impending downsizing because you cannot conceive that it could affect you
- When a man says that he's always been faithful because affairs out of town don't count
- When a person smoking a cigarette says she is not a smoker because she bummed this cigarette instead of buying it

Denial is what allows you to skip the condom, despite a decade of safe-sex lectures, or to have another drink for the road, despite blood-alcohol lectures. Denial is what makes it so hard to learn from our mistakes.

Unlike "self-discipline," which has a dated flavor, "denial" has definitely become a fashionable piece of self-awareness. To be "in denial" means to deceive yourself about the extent of or damage done by your addictive behavior. Popularized by the recovery movement, it is most useful as a phrase that comforts friends and family who cannot understand how two car accidents and evidence of vomit on one's shoes are not proof enough of a drinking problem ("He's in denial").

To some degree we all rely on denial to get us through the night. It helps us avoid anxiety and enjoy hope, even if it is sometimes false hope. Love's delusion allows you to think your child's poor school performance means he is brilliant but bored, or to believe that if your married lover left his wife he would certainly be faithful to you. Each is a form of denial.

In a sense, denial can even enhance your power because it is a version of courage. It may cause you to overstate your strengths and deny your limitations and so accomplish great things. Think of the realities Lance Armstrong needed to deny in order to set his sights on the Tour de France after cancer treatment, or the personal limitations to which Katharine Graham needed to blind herself in order to take over *The Washington Post*. When it helps you avoid self-defeating anxiety, denial is a treasured ally. It's a great defense, and a necessary one, but like every distortion, denial may soothe anxiety at the price of your problem-solving abilities.

When you are creating conflict or putting yourself at risk, denial is a dead end. President Clinton left us that indelible portrait of compartmentalization and denial, sitting at his desk receiving oral sex from the waist down and on the phone talking politics from the waist up. A little less lockbox and a little more capacity to see the whole could have made him act in his own interests more effectively—not to mention our own. Denial made it impossible for him to act in his own best interests.

Denial has an ugly stepsister, a mirror image if you will, that takes the form of fantasy. If denial solves problems by pretending they don't exist, fantasy solves them by pretending solutions will simply, effortlessly appear. Like denial, fantasy has its positive face, especially when it is used to fuel constructive visions of how change might be possible. Most often, though, fantasy is only avoidance, gift wrapped.

It's easy to spot the dodge of fantasy in someone else—easy and often frustrating. For example, a friend approached me on behalf of his sister. "How can I help her?" he asks. "Her husband's a real bastard and my sister sits around and cries. She'll call me, with every damn miserable thing he does—he made fun of her to his mother, he wouldn't dream of helping with the baby, he comes and goes as he pleases, but she has to report in every few hours. She gets freaked out if she forgets to turn on her cell phone, because maybe he tried to get her and he'll be furious.

"Then, instead of getting in his face with all this stuff, she'll start playing his shrink, figuring why he's so difficult. His father was controlling; his mother was a witch; she wounded his self-esteem. Who gives a shit, is what I want to know. My sister even thinks her husband's jealousy is proof that he loves her, and since he loves her, well—someday, some way—she'll have a happy ending.

"If I disagree, she defends him. She starts arguing. Things will definitely get better—when his job improves, when he makes more money and feels better about himself, when she's able to get pregnant again and he stops resenting her for staying home. But she won't do anything to make them better. She won't consider leaving him, won't confront him, won't even stick up for herself because it 'just makes him madder.'

"What can I do for my sister?" asks my friend.

Frankly, nothing. My friend's sister is deep in the comfort of a rescue fantasy and doing nothing is precisely its point.

This is the heart of a comfort zone's allure. What we want most is not to act. Not to dislodge ourselves, not to endure the discomfort of movement, the anxiety of change. At the same time, we want something else, something more, something just over the wall. We know what we need to do, but we avoid doing it because it hurts; we distract ourselves by laying the blame elsewhere for our pain, or by denying that pain altogether.

Finally, ultimately, we daydream about rescue. What you or I or this sister seek may be very different, but we share the fantasy that some essential change will be delivered to us and we won't have to move from our comfort zone at all. That fantasy is the fourth great cul-de-sac into which some people disappear for a lifetime.

We are waiting for that delivery. Our job or lover or parent or child will change and then we will be happy or free. We are specific about how that person or situation should change to delight us; we may have communicated those hopes and expectations on more than one occasion. We have certainly assembled our arguments as to why we are entitled to these changes, deserving of this satisfaction or that support.

The conviction—my life will be better when something changes, but that something depends on someone else—feels so completely true that it takes a very long time to recognize it for the fantasy it is. In fact, we don't call it rescue or fantasy at all. In our hearts, these are our just desserts.

Now, like my friend's sister, and like Lydia, we are waiting to be served.

Lydia's current comfort zone—lifer, private weaver, city dweller, single, isolated, safe—offers her plenty of security and little of the life satisfaction she craves. She needs to peek out of the fantasy and denial caves and take a look at her uncomfortable realities.

How do I get her to do that? How do you get yourself to do it? How do any of us overcome the insidious lures of denial and fantasy? By inching, edging, backing into, sliding sideways toward those hurtful truths. And then, sometimes, by being clubbed over the head with them.

To Tell the Truth

The medicine for denial and fantasy is objective fact and a willingness to see. Sometimes that's enough.

Sometimes, though, it's no help at all. You cannot force someone else out of denial, though you can make it more uncomfortable to stay in:

Tell your girlfriend that her husband propositioned you at the last party and she may decide you are no friend at all. Have you pierced her marital bubble? Maybe, but only to the degree that she herself is willing to face what hurts.

An internist may tell her patient that the chest X-ray shows some troubling lung spots. Those facts may break through that patient's hazy "it'll never happen to me" defense that allows her to light up two packs a day. But it's no guarantee.

Do the research and you may discover that only one person out of fifty ever gets tenure at your university, or gets promoted from your department of the company, or makes it from the minors to the majors in your sport. Facing these sore spots could help you put together a smart professional backup plan. Or you might just use them to sink into a trough of blame—these institutions are so unfair and here you are, victimized again. Or you might ignore the facts altogether, cross your fingers, and wait to bowl a strike.

Facts, though, do make both denial and fantasy more difficult to maintain. Creep out of your cave and confront reality by marshaling whatever objective data are relevant to your unhappy situation. Facts—how long, how much, how frequent, how does it compare to others, what is statistically the most likely outcome, or what is your best intuitive bet—function as pushpins, skewering your problem to the bulletin board at the front of your consciousness. From there, with your full attention, you are far more likely to solve it.

Over the course of several sessions I determined to present Lydia with the full picture of pregnancy and adoption possibilities for a woman her age. For one thing, her situation was the subject of any number of cover stories, and our failure to discuss it seemed to me a fine example of denial. For another, I believe that Lydia has strengths she has yet to muster. Facts might serve as a catalyst to mobilize that strength for whatever decision she might make.

I gave Lydia several articles on fertility from popular magazines, a list of suggested books, the names of two reputable fertility specialists and one adoption consultant. Lydia found this forced recitation upsetting. The problem feels more daunting when you look at it objectively. Well, of course it does, that's why you've been avoiding it. Denial and fantasy are soap bubble cushions. Facts that pierce the bubble let you down with a jolt.

I chose to confront the motherhood piece of Lydia's vision because time made it the most pressing issue, but I could just have reasonably chosen to discuss real estate prices, rentals, and job prospects in Bucks County, because these facts, too, might have galvanized Lydia into action. Objective information might have made Lydia change her investment strategy, or review her professional options, for example. In each case, I would be using data to crack Lydia's denial and pierce her rescue fantasy, hoping objective evidence might point her in the direction of a life plan, where denial and fantasy were leaving her stuck in the rut she told me she was starting to furnish.

In exactly the same way that discipline needs to be paired with the deliberate summoning of courage, facing facts needs to be accompanied by constant reassurance and self-soothing. You will need to coax, support, and reassure yourself through any recitation of hard truth. These new truths will hurt, that's why you've been avoiding them. But once you see what you have long ignored, *remind yourself there is something you can do about it.* You have the ability to face an anxiety and overcome it.

Lydia could make decisions about single motherhood—about foreign adoption, fertility treatment, frozen eggs, or foster parenting, mentoring, big sister programs, or a number of other ways to become a parent or surrogate parent. But she couldn't make any of those decisions as long as she was in denial.

Similarly, Jack benefited by recognizing his part in raising Jane's hopes for marriage, even if such recognition initially made him squirm. It helped him identify and resolve his own conflicted desire rather than viewing himself as "forced" by Jane or some other woman.

Ryan agreed to keep a log of his marijuana use, just to get an objective measure of the amount of time he spent stoned as compared to the amount of time he spent doing the hard tasks required to further his long-term goals. The point of the log was to crack through his denial and reflect back his actual life.

You reap what you sow. Ryan wasn't planting much in the way of a path to self-respect, and his current comfort zone was never going to deliver that. If he stops getting high, if he stops blaming his grandfather and the family in general, if he stops ignoring his own bad habits, he will start to face what hurts. Then he can make something happen. But what?

So can you, but what?

CHAPTER 4

CREATE A VISION

A particularly reflective woman describes her own comfort zone jailbreak:

In the tenth year of my marriage, I had a recurring image. I saw myself locked in a tall tower that had only one window. I hated to look out that window and see everything I was missing, but I was drawn to it, too. Half of me wanted to brick the window over so I could be satisfied where I was, and half of me wanted to just jump out. I was always trying to make the tower nicer— redecorating it, having another child, having a more loving attitude.

I used to imagine that I'd be rescued and in a way I was. I fell in love with another man and I eventually left the tower to live with him. It really meant destroying the whole tower, pulling it down around me, and that was god-awful. But it was worth it.

When I think of it now I see that, while I was rescued, it was because I was hanging out that window and waving frantically to everyone that passed, "Hey, I'm up here. Come and get me."

It's said you need to "see it to be it," and in my experience that's true. No matter how much it hurts where you are, without the vision of something better, you're not going anywhere.

The pain where you are and the motivating power of your vision of change coexist in a tricky balance. If you are in emotional agony, you are apt to flee a comfort zone going toward nothing more than an escape from that pain. That's how people quit dreadful jobs without arranging for an alternative. Likewise, if your discomfort is minimal but enormous desire sweeps you, that passionate vision may pull you toward it, regardless of how cozy your current comfort zone may be. That's how people leave decent, dull spouses for sexual liaisons.

But most of us are like the woman in the tower. Discomfort with where we are has to join with something we see through the window, and we only look through the window because we are uncomfortable where we are. Both elements are essential, or we end up staying put. The problem is, the devil we know is powerful enough reassurance to roast any of us over familiar coals indefinitely. Our signals of emotional pain need to combine with some beacon, some prize, or we will cling to that comfort trap forever.

Consider these situations:

Frances will never leave her alcoholic boyfriend until she has an optimistic view of life without him. As long as she pictures herself doomed to loneliness, she will stay in the relationship and continue cataloging his every abuse for any friend who is still willing to listen.

Gwen will never enjoy the new opportunities afforded by her husband's financial success as long as she envisions herself left out by a world of skinny social snobs. She'll stay nestled in her old house, clinging to her old routine, perhaps even patting herself on the back for resisting money's corrupting influence. Her husband, though, wants to enjoy his success with new toys, new people, new experiences. He pushes, she pulls back, and so they grow farther apart.

Will discovered in his first year of law school that he found the law a tedious business. But without a spark in some other direction, he will live and die a captive lawyer. Unhappy as he is in his career, he is also *comfortable*. With nothing better to counter it, the inertia of his comfort zone will prevail.

For many, picturing something better is the simplest step. You know what's missing, you know what hurts, and you can see exactly what prize or possibility would make tolerating the anxiety of change worth your while. For you, step two is easy.

A motivating vision, though, does not always emerge of its own accord. Nor does it have to. You can think one up, image by image or goal by goal. Whether consciously developed or born unbidden out of overwhelming desire, that vision is still a product of your heart and mind—and therein lies its power.

The form of those motivating visions is individual. They can be vivid mental images or only the vague outlines of a plan. They can be inspiring beliefs, whether in oneself or some higher power. Yours might take the form of a well-defined goal, or it might be closer to a moment of insight, a flash of hope or disgust that double-clicks on your brain and opens up another path.

Whether your own vision takes the form of a structured goal, intuitive leap, vivid mental image, or spiritual calling, certain common elements will be true:

- *It must be positive.* You need to go toward something rewarding, not simply away from something unpleasant. "I don't want to be angry all the time" becomes "I see myself calm and at peace." "This job will never pay me what I'm worth" holds you unhappily in place. "I believe I will find a job that will pay me more" moves you forward.

- *It must be under your control.* Most of our comfort zones would be improved if something or someone else would change. We want bosses who appreciate us, boyfriends who will commit, wives who complain less, and friends who apologize first. As much time as you may spend imagining these pleasant additions to your life, they are not what is meant by creating a vision. Each of these fantasies requires that someone else leave his or her comfort zone. A motivating vision is the payoff you hope to receive *if you leave yours.*

- *It has to move you forward, if only a step.* This last is the most surprising truth. A motivating vision does not have to solve your entire problem. It just needs to inspire enough forward motion to get you unstuck or give you a different perspective on things.

When we leave a comfort zone, many of us don't know exactly where we are going to end up. Sometimes we need to circle around a little, take a temporary detour. We leave the stifling job for a year in the Peace Corps or a season selling hot dogs at the beach. It's true we're postponing the long-term career question, but sometimes just experiencing someplace new, if only in the short run, may help you take that further leap to a fresh comfort zone months down the road.

Big decisions may be too overwhelming to make all at once, and so we inch toward them. We can't see ourselves leaving the marriage, don't even know if we want to leave the marriage. But we can imagine shifting the marital balance a bit by going back to school or taking a part-time job or beginning to manage the investments. We take these half steps out of a comfort zone without knowing in advance how much change might follow, or what direction that change might take.

Jack, for example, took his half step when he went to St. Croix. He could only see that far down the road, but it turned out to be far enough. He put himself in a new, positive situation with new ground rules. He wasn't ready to resolve his conflict, but he did move past his earlier constrictions. That's all it takes.

As long as your vision is positive, is under your control, and serves as sufficient exit strategy from your current comfort zone, don't worry about whether it has resolved your entire dilemma. New ground will give you new outcomes.

Follow Karin's story, and you'll see how the path from your comfort zone to higher ground might circle back to yourself.

What's in a Vision?

Karin tosses herself into her three o'clock appointment, distributing huge smiles and shopping bags around the office before climaxing into a chair. She usually begins her session with a swift anecdote told for my entertainment, so I settle back to enjoy it.

"On the way here I hit every red light and my ex-husband's divorce lawyer."

"Actually hit him?"

"Fender to bender, doll."

"Was there any serious damage?"

"No. But there will be. He asked me out for dinner and I said I'd go."

"Right. Uh, Karin, one thing, you've never been married, have you?"

"OK, ex-boyfriend. Your point?"

"Shall we begin?"

Anecdote sufficiently appreciated, Karin then arranges her coffee, water bottle, bagel bag, and Altoid tin like Stations of the Cross around her. These props provide her necessary avoidance totems should my questions or her own feelings become too pointed. I was trained to insist that people dispense with distractions during a psychotherapy session. Feelings are, after all, more easily understood when they are not choked back by a bagel. Twenty-five years of practice have mostly taught me when to ignore my training. I do not insist that Karin face me unprotected. At least not yet.

In unexpected contrast to her sense of personal theater, Karin has a dour and rigorous job as vice president and European sales director for a multinational software company. She speaks fast in three languages and can say enough to make you laugh in two others. She's a brain cake frosted with sugary blond sex. I imagine that her extreme combination of classic hysteric emotional life and obsessive-compulsive intellect has left quite a wake through her personal relationships, but we've yet to thoroughly discuss it. Karin is focused instead on the details of her most immediate crisis.

At thirty-six, she is engaged to Marshall, a sweetheart of a mergers and acquisitions specialist, if such a thing is possible. Yet just before they became engaged, Karin began having an affair with an older, married partner in her firm, whom she calls "Doctor Bob" because "he's such an operator," ha, ha, ha. Her anxiety about this affair makes Karin feel that she is slowly self-destructing.

Karin and her fiancé, Marshall, have been together three years, and Karin describes him with affection and admiration as "a very, very good man." Dr. Bob, on the other hand, is not a particularly good man, but he is "totally my type"—by which Karin apparently means a senior son-of-a-bitch whose allure is the perfume of arrogance. Karin is a drop-dead sucker for arrogance. Once she gets a whiff, she wants to be that boy's special girl.

Initially I thought Karin was presenting a female version of the classic madonna/whore conflict so common to my male patients. Nice boy/bad boy—oh God, let me have a bit of both. Nothing about that dilemma is easily sorted out, but the issue is at least fairly circumscribed. But as I got to know Karin, I understood that I was, as usual, oversimplifying.

Two sessions into my conversation with Karin and I was mentally playing her song, "It's Raining Men"—no added "hallelujah." Marshall and Dr. Bob were only the lead players in Karin's current drama. In fact, there were male bit players, walk-ons, supporting figures—there were old lovers, possible lovers, one-night stands whose feelings she wanted to spare. "I wouldn't call it rape," she said of one encounter with the cousin of a friend, who pushed her down on a hotel bed and forced her legs apart. "I would call it not having the heart or the guts to say 'no' loud enough. It was so important to him and, really, it was nothing to me."

And everywhere there were men, there was Karin. Pleasing, wooing, seducing, charming, connecting, sucking, and sweet-talking. Eleven years in the technology industry—outstanding professional record, by the way, told to me as pure aside and only after I asked directly—left Karin's life littered with men. It seems she is drawn to this male world and is perfectly capable of competing with men on their own turf. It's just that, whether she wins or loses, Karin somehow always has to make it up to the guys by soothing them sexually. Karin lets herself be conquered, almost as an obligation to make the men around her feel better about themselves.

They probably do, but the price to Karin is high. She loves and longs for children, but she's had an abortion. The pregnancy was not greeted positively by the prospective father and she could never envision herself defying her partner's wishes enough to have the baby. Karin is tortured by self-hatred, both regarding the abortion and because of the pain her infidelity will cause her fiancé.

The intensity of her emotions has made it difficult for Karin to successfully avoid what hurts, though she tends to get caught in the loop of self-blame rather than face the tough choice ahead. When she does look forward, she sees her problem as a choice between two men—a "good" fiancé and a "bad" lover whom she ought to abandon, though somehow she can't. Karen feels safe pleasing men, but it's dangerous to please herself. She's in a comfort zone that is becoming increasingly uncomfortable.

In many ways Karin's situation is the opposite of what you

may have come to think of as being stuck in a comfort zone. Neither safe nor stale, Karin's life is, instead, dramatic, intense, and eventful. There are daily near misses—cell phone numbers improperly disguised, late-night office clutches with doors only partially shut, parked-car passions that send her home to Marshall in gummy underwear. How can any of this be described as comfortable?

Your comfort zone is comfortable in the sense that it is familiar, that it "fits," that it feels like you. It's comfortable because it re-creates an internal state that feels safe and/or satisfying. Surely Karin's ongoing anxiety could not be described as a feeling of safety. So what is there in this triangle she has created that could possibly be experienced as satisfying?

Well, sex for a start, and she does describe Dr. Bob as a hell of a lover. She's hooked on his approval, too, and on his pleasure. She imagines he could have anyone and he has chosen her, which stirs in her a high of pride and excitement to which Marshall has never moved her.

Still, there is a tense uncertainty to her relationship with Dr. Bob. He withdraws unaccountably, becomes cold and distant and then responsive by inexplicable turns. This erratic reward system works on Karin exactly as it does in a psychology lab when a lab rat gets the food pellet at random intervals. The rat stands pushing the bar frantically, never knowing when he might be rewarded. Karin is similarly hooked.

Karin's comfort zone offers her the intense satisfaction of wooing and pleasing Dr. Bob, and it also offers her the security of Marshall's devotion. The two men together provide an overwhelming sense of satisfaction and security, but they are a combustible combination. Karin clearly fears that she will lose them both and be left with nothing. She is guilty, anxious, confused, and, as she describes it, utterly trapped in the mess she feels she's making of her own life.

Let's eliminate the obvious exits right off the bat. Hey, dump the philanderer, marry Mr. Nice Guy, and have his babies. Call me crazy—could anything be simpler? Karin, whose intelligence really is ferocious, does not need me to point out this solution. She knows what she should do; she's just not doing it. Karin is here in my office because she can see that her house is on fire, but she's sitting around inside, toasting marshmallows. Why won't she flee for her life? The thrill, it seems, is in the burn.

What might move Karin to take action, short of the explosion of discovery? Without the affair's discovery, Karin is likely to initiate a change only if she is able to take the first two steps: She has to face what hurts—namely that she must make a painful choice that will require her to let go of something precious. Then, however tentatively, she'll need to create some positive vision of how that painful choice might turn out well.

However much it hurts where she is, Karin will need a vision of something better to go toward in order to move forward. As Karin sorted through her guilt and anxiety in order to face what hurt, we began to focus on her vision of a possible future. We know how she feels. What we don't know is what she is going to do about it. (Push. Push. I am coaching myself. Push. Just don't push so hard that you push her out the door.)

Over and over I direct Karin toward the same question: What would she do if she weren't afraid? If she could choose for herself, if she could speak her truth, if she could totally control the outcome here, what would she make happen? What does she *desire*?

Desire is the psychic juice that contributes two essential elements to your vision: both the raw material from which to create that vision *and* the emotional energy, the driving force with which to pursue it. Without desire, your vision would be only static imagery, absent the magnetic pull that coaxes you to take risks and face fear. Without that concrete vision, though, your desire may be reduced to a restless, unfocused yearning.

Think of the vision you create as a concrete expression of your heart's desire. Desire and its vision: You yearn for sexual satisfaction and so picture yourself initiating sex with your husband and telling him clearly what would please you. You hunger for recognition and so set a long-term strategy for election to the National Board in your profession. You want to please your father, and so decide to win the same crew race he won at your age. You compete furiously with your younger sister, and so determine to marry a man richer than her husband. You long for girlfriends who will understand your new-mommy angst, and so start up a playgroup with some promising acquaintances.

Remember, not every desire you satisfy is an honorable or admirable one. Your desire may be noble or ugly, limp or raging beyond reason; the vision you produce to express that desire may be partial and dim or as detailed as a Disney animation. But the two—desire and vision—must be paired to work their magic.

A positive vision is created by recognizing desire and conjuring its satisfaction. Like Karin, then, when you confront your own stuck spot, begin with the questions What would I do if I weren't afraid? What do I want?

As soon as you ask the questions, you'll notice you've hit a problem. Frequently, the voice of your desire is not the inspiring solo of love song or sonnet. It might more closely resemble the bickering chorus of sitcom characters.

You want to stay married, but you dream of divorce; you want to stand up for yourself but have the whole office like you; you support your child's independence but want to maintain control. From which of these urges will you form your vision?

You want wealth and professional satisfaction, but you don't want to work very hard for them. Does that mean you don't really want them?

You want desperately to binge eat, but you have learned to fight that desire for your own well-being. If you resist this destructive passion, what positive inner light will guide you?

Karin wants two men, so how can desire direct her?

Desire—clear, positive, focused, brightly burning—is the fuel necessary to propel any of us across a tightrope of anxiety onto new emotional territory. It only stands to reason.

But desire is not reasonable. Desire is complicated, shadowy, with paradoxes of its own. It's true that you've got to want something before you can muster the strength to go get it. But wanting is a funny thing. It is only partly conscious, it is rarely wholehearted, it is barely rational, and, even with all these caveats, it is one of life's most compelling forces. Desire is the siren song.

Why You Don't Know What You Want

This second step requires that you "create a positive vision." Sometimes, in fact, that vision finds you. Desire can attack and thereby bring all the walls tumbling down. My patient Ruth, the one who regained all that weight before she faced her fear of dating, had this experience once in her life. I think that is part of what she guards against now.

"This sounds outrageous but here's what happened. I was sitting in an office lobby after a job interview, pretty pleased because I'd gotten the job. A man walked by, then stopped and looked at me. I didn't know him, I don't think I had ever seen him before. I started to smile at him and I thought, 'Holy shit. I'm in trouble.' Because I knew I had to know him, had to sleep with him, pretty much had to have him. I didn't even *know* him, but that's how I felt. He told me later he walked past me and thought, 'She looks easy.'

"I was married, he was married, he even had a child. It didn't make any difference. I went home and spent that whole weekend in bed because I knew I would see him at that office on Monday. I brought in a book of poetry for him that first day, and I just went after him. I have to say we both went through hell, with an out-of-control office affair, leaving our spouses, ending up together.

"We married about four years after that thunderbolt, and had our son two years later. I interpreted our passion to mean we were meant to be together. He interpreted it to mean he was a hell of a stud. Finally I got the friendly-fire phone call, the one that goes 'I just thought you'd want to know . . .' He was having yet another office affair. I threw him out and ended up raising our son alone. End of love story. End of men."

End of desire? What a relief.

Certainly, as many thunderbolts of desire end happily ever after as end in devastation. And as many are linked to a sense of purpose as to a sense of passion—creating driving visions of career choice, religious commitment, or profound life change. People who experience such compelling desire know firsthand how its seductive power can draw them out of a comfort zone and across minefields of anxiety to reach an envisioned reward.

Such pure, unfettered, burning desire, though, rarely comes

into my office. I am more apt to meet conflicted desire, half-hearted ambition, guilty impulse, "yes, buts," "on the other hands," and brokenhearted frustration. I counsel many with insufficient desire, coach people to stand up against their destructive desires, and try to help them make peace with unfulfilled desires.

But pure and passionate desire itself, the real unadulterated stuff, is the uncut heroin of the soul. You just don't find it on the streets. Most of us make do with some watered-down version with which to fuel our forward motion. Under the proper circumstances, though, and with enough of your conscious self in your own corner, that diluted version will be more than enough. That's the most important thing to remember as you create your own vision.

Recognizing that something hurts, that you need to break free of your own comfort zone, you'll ask yourself, *What do I want?* Your initial answer may well be a resounding *Jeez, I don't know.*

Well, you sort of know, but you're not sure. You are torn between desires, or reluctant to want what you feel sure you can't have, or want something one day and turn your back on it the next. Or you thought you knew what you wanted but you sure aren't doing what you need to get it, so perhaps you don't want it after all? Conflict, ambivalence, frustration, depression, and sometimes just your better judgment each diminish the clarity of desire.

You will move through the fiery ring of anxiety that surrounds your comfort zone by keeping your eyes on the prize. But that prize can easily get lost in the fog of internal debate or despair. You will create a clearer and more powerful vision for yourself if you recognize the likely obstacles currently obscuring your view.

The key here is to recognize those internal obstacles, not neces-

sarily to resolve them. Each of the internal obstacles we'll discuss is a perfectly natural, if difficult, part of the human condition. Yes, you have to want something badly enough to force yourself to face change. But you can want it humanly, with hesitation, recognizing it as a mixed blessing. If you are a thinking adult, that may be the only way you are going to be able to want something that is going to change your life in some unknown way.

I point this out because many peppy motivational guides advise us to be single-minded in pursuit of change, littering our desks with Post-its of pithy reminders like, "It doesn't matter how distant the goal, as long as every step you take is in that direction." This piece of advice is unarguable, but also irrelevant. I have rarely met someone utterly committed to the unknown, and that is what change is. I imagine even Neil Armstrong had a second thought or two before he stepped out onto the moon. The point is, he went anyway.

We create a new vision, despite the part of us that disputes that goal; we move forward, despite the part of us that wants to stay under the covers.

Still, simply recognizing which forces cloud your vision actually helps to clarify things. Generally speaking, there are five ways to dilute desire: conflict, ambivalence, frustration, addiction, and suppression.

Conflict—I Want Two Things and I Can't Have Them Both

"I'm out of control," Karin says with real fear. "I'm out of my mind," though she proves she is not with her perfect grasp of the potential wreckage ahead. Why am I not more guilty? she

wonders. Why am I risking everything? I have a great relationship and I am throwing it away. "Stop me," she tells me in some
sessions. "Stop me because I can't stop myself." And then she
adds: "Don't get in my way. I want this. I have to have him. This
feels too good, too good. I can't be without it. Don't you dare try
to stop me."

Conflicting desire for two men, each satisfying different
needs, makes it seem impossible for Karin to create a vision of
where to go from here. Either imagined choice is bleak, conjuring painful loss rather than positive gain. Without that positive
vision to move toward, Karin can only try to satisfy both conflicting impulses—pursuing her lover while protecting her relationship as best she can. Enduring the internal conflict, though, is
torture. Eventually she will have to choose or, far more likely,
live with the choice forced on her by one of the other participants in her drama. Meanwhile, she stays where she is and suf-
fers accordingly.

What happens if outside pressures don't force you to choose
between conflicting desires? What if Karin's lover and her fiancé
both endure the status quo for reasons of their own? What if Jane
had never pressed Jack to divorce his fantasy and marry her?
What if Ryan dithers between a plan to expand his family's business and his longtime fantasy of owning a sports bar, all the while
collecting a paycheck? How do conflicting desires resolve into a
unified motivating vision, when the world doesn't do the choosing for you?

Sometimes they don't.

Sometimes you choose anyway.

Sometimes you find a third option or take a half step. And it's
enough.

When nothing shifts and your conflicting desires pin you in

place, you will wait, as Karin has been doing, until the world acts upon you. Your unconscious might lend a hand, though, leaving the love letters in the open briefcase where they are easier for your wife to find; miscalculating your birth control when you can't decide whether you want that third child; forgetting to set the alarm when your detestable boss fires people who are late. Certainly Karin has been dribbling hints to Marshall despite her own conscious efforts to protect him. Still, unless he or Bob acts, Karin might just churn in the same comfort zone indefinitely. If your own desires are in conflict, you, too, might wait until the world chooses for you.

On the other hand, you might gather your inner resources and act. Two mutually exclusive desires—Bob and Marshall, Jane and sexual freedom, the family business and freedom from family—may be temporarily difficult, but they don't have to be terminally paralyzing. You'll want one option more, or the imagined loss of the other will hurt less, or you have a strong value system or moral precept that guides your difficult choices. You make a rational assessment or get a glimpse of heaven and one or the other moves you forward against all the reasons keeping you in place.

Finally, you might discover, as Karin did, that some third option offers the most motivating vision for personal progress. As you'll see in the second half of this chapter, Karin resolves her conflict between two men by looking inward and defining her vision in terms of herself instead of her partners. Perhaps such a third option might work for you, too.

Internal conflict does not have be totally resolved, but to the degree that it is not, your motivating desire is watered down by a huge *but*. That *but*, if it's loud enough, can disable you in the all-too-familiar aggravated whine of ambivalence.

Ambivalence—I Want It and I Don't Want It

Ambivalence is the emotional smear that blurs your focus. This feature of inner conflict is such special torture to those of us in its familiar claw that it merits separate discussion. Hamlet is our literary model; Mario Cuomo is our poster child. Your own ambivalence may center on more pedestrian concerns than becoming king or believing you are one, but it can nonetheless sap desire and fog your vision. For example:

I want an honest relationship, but I don't want to stop sneaking the things that make my partner mad.

I want to retire, but I don't want to see myself as a retiree.

Or, as in Karin's case, I want to marry Marshall, but maybe I'd be bored with Marshall.

Ambivalence is such a simple, common, nearly universal experience. Why does it always seem to sneak up on my patients kamikaze-like, leaving them devastated by its emotional power and paralyzed to act before its implacable punishments of doubt and dread? In part it's because we were not prepared for it, taught the opposite, in fact. "You'll know when it's right," we're told, although frequently we know no such thing. "Trust your gut," we are advised, which works except for the occasions when your gut twists in knots of ambivalence.

Finally, ambivalence is tough because it puts us face to face with the cost of a decision. Conscious ambivalence allows you to see and feel what you are giving up. Some of us allow that ouch to stop us in our tracks indefinitely. Others bear down, pay the price, and after some inevitable hesitation, prod themselves to move on.

How do you nudge yourself toward a vision dimmed by your

conflicting feelings? ("Aye, there's the rub.") To create a stronger vision you need to learn to tolerate ambivalence, appreciate its payoffs, or take action that will reduce its power.

Learning to tolerate ambivalence means recognizing, with affection, that it is your own natural state, if not in all issues then in some key ones. You may never feel totally committed to a vision of leaving your job to be a full-time mother, or leaving your child to return to work. But you can motivate yourself to make these necessary changes by recognizing that conflicted is simply the way you are going to feel. Sometimes you need to challenge your comfort zone with a heavy heart. That ambivalence doesn't have to mean you are making the wrong move. It may only mean that you are making a grown-up move and not all of those are cleanly decided.

Friends of mine provided a terrific model for tolerating ambivalence when they explained how they resolved their endless city/suburbs debate. First they obsessed for two years over the pros and cons of moving to the suburbs. Finally they made the move, only to discover that, instead of it being a peaceful resolution, they had instead begun a family debate about the pros and cons of moving back to the city, exhausting themselves and several real estate agents through their interminable waffling. I asked them recently how they were feeling about their dilemma. "Oh," explained the wife, "it got much better when we accepted that we are chronic malcontents. Once we realized we aren't going to be happy anywhere, it was much easier to stay where we are."

Affectionate self-awareness is medicine for many psychic ills.

Appreciating the subtle rewards of ambivalence may make it less of an obstacle, too. For example, especially in romantic relationships, ambivalence gives you the upper hand. Marshall wants Karin, but Karin is still deciding on Marshall. Jane wants Jack, but Jack is still deciding on Jane. True, the uncertainty that Karin and Jack and maybe you, too, are experiencing is not pleasant. But it is powerful, protecting you from all the vulnerabilities to which committed love exposes us. Recognizing that you may be clinging to ambivalence for your own protection can help reduce your confusion about what you desire.

Finally, action partly resolves ambivalence. Face what hurts in your current comfort zone and move toward your new vision, despite your mixed feelings, and sometimes that movement alone shifts your focus. Jack's story is an example of how action can create a sense of resolution. With the question of marriage behind him, he could become the proud husband, though when that question was before him he could only be the Hamlet of bachelors.

Tolerance, appreciation, and action may each reduce ambivalence, but when we are in its throes, we don't have the full force of desire to propel us toward our heart's desire. Instead of desire, what we feel is frustration.

Frustration—I Know What I Want, but I Can't Seem to Get It

Three cold-call failures—and I don't want to be in sales anymore.

Two bad blind dates—and I give up on that whole Internet dating torture.

Discover I need to complete course requirements before I can even apply for vet school—so I want to abandon the whole vet fantasy.

Gained a pound this week—so the Weight Watchers thing isn't worth sticking with.

Vision. Obstacle. Frustration. Now what?

I told you it was going to be a fight.

Between you and any envisioned goal there are likely to be obstacles. When those obstacles bar your way, you feel frustrated. Now the interesting question is, What happens to your desire for the goal?

The impact of that frustration on your desire is as illogical as desire itself. For example, when a desired goal is out of your control—getting your teenager to keep a clean room, for example, or getting your husband to stop eating junk food—many people will endure years of frustration without even considering abandoning the goal. Family relationships suffer, the bad habits remain entrenched, yet no amount of frustration causes this wife or parent to abandon her goal. I am tempted to conclude that we are least affected by frustration when the goal we desire requires someone else to change.

When it is our own comfort zone we are being asked to abandon, however, frustration has a much swifter impact on desire. Like Ryan's hurt refusal to pursue business discussions in the face of his family's lack of confidence, many of our own desires fall to frustration without our even staging a proper burial. Left without a vision, we stay where we are. Good or bad, it's comfortable.

Your threshold for frustration and your ability to tolerate frustration when you reach that threshold are key to leaving your comfort zone. Remember, desire is your gas. We inch our way out of a comfort zone because, and only because, we are moving toward something better (even if, for sure, we can't perfectly articulate what that something better is). Like conflict and ambivalence, frustration is a factor that may diminish desire to a point where its fuel is useless.

The opposite is true, too. Sometimes desire is so loud, so riveting, that every part of you is engaged in withstanding its typhoon force. When you are, there is nothing subtle about the fight you are in. It's a battle for self-preservation.

Addiction—I Want It, but It's Destroying Me

Consider this ironic illogic of desire: Envision self-improvement, commit to exercise, and the slight impediment of a rainy walk to the gym may derail your entire workout program. But get a self-destructive craving for cocaine or an ice cream binge and you will drive five miles in a blizzard for a fix. Why might that be?

Maybe it's because self-improvement requires that you go to the edge of your comfort zone and beyond, while the addictive fix gives you instant short-term comfort right where you are. Such is the power of comfort, and that is what you are pushing against.

Think of addiction as an extreme version of a comfort zone, kind of your comfort zone on steroids. You will need to follow the same seven-step path to the exit. But each step is more wrenching because your addiction magnifies your comfort zone such that a bright vision of life without it seems impossible to conjure.

I am using "addiction" here in the broadest possible context, to refer to any harmful substance, habit, or even person whom you are definitely going to give up on Monday, if you could only have just a few more days of the pleasure it affords. Whether it is a cigarette, an abusive lover, or a drink, you already know it's an utterly empty comfort trap. But picturing life without it is bleak.

Imagine yourself without that drink, the cigarette, that lover and you will have to struggle to see that emptiness in a positive light. Yet your ability to create such a positive vision—to see yourself with your morning coffee and no cigarette, *smiling and relaxed*; to envision yourself *calmly, confidently* packing to leave the lover who is promising to change; to imagine yourself laughing at a party with nothing stronger than a Diet Coke in your hand—is a critical element in stable recovery.

That positive vision is usually not sufficient to battle addiction, whose tenacious force may require group support, physical rehabilitation, medication, and other resources before it can be beaten back. But a positive vision is an absolutely necessary element. Step two: Create a Vision may be your toughest move. You will be fighting against addiction's power to squelch all other desires.

Just as we have a natural human impulse to stay comfortable, so we have a paradoxical impulse toward growth and change—an energy whose power may allow us to conquer even ferocious addictions. Nothing so successfully keeps us in place, however, as when that natural human desire for growth is suppressed.

Suppression—I Don't Know What I Want

Early on, Lydia recounted to me this conversation with an acquaintance:

"What's up?" Lydia asked.

"I'm just great," said the friend. "I sold the West Coast branch of my company because I wanted to focus on one place and do graduate school, so one night a week I fly into Boston for a part-time organizational development master's program. Oh, and I met this great guy on the plane. You know, I thought I'd be really lonely after my divorce, but that's going great. What about you?"

"I got a cat."

"Boredom," Tolstoy said, "is the desire for desire." That absence of desire will paste you in your familiar place as much as any anxiety. However flat or painful your comfort zone may be, when you look across the psychological horizon and nothing beckons, you stay put.

Tolstoy might say that your horse died of boredom. I would suggest that you are just taking cover. Desire is a life spark, a natural hunger. Like every other appetite, it can be temporarily squelched.

The very same distractions that prevent us from facing what hurts will certainly also suppress desire. Bingeing on any substance, whether television, alcohol, drugs, food, or music, can induce a trancelike state in which desire is not so much sated as evaporated. What is there to want? Who knows? Therefore, what is there to risk? Not much.

After avoidance, depression—that whole huge syndrome of racking, involuntary retreat—is probably the single greatest suppressant of desire. Depression is an umbrella term describing a mood arc from fully functioning sadness to absolute physical and mental paralysis. That's a very long slide, measured by an ever-increasing loss of energy on the way down. As energy ebbs when your mood turns bleak, desire recedes, if only to make it possible to hunker down in your safe cave and recover.

Depression, even in its moderate forms, will suppress more than your desire for change or your capacity to envision it. It can be a lethal blanket, smothering your ability to work, to concentrate, to sleep or eat, to savor pleasure, or to love. An unsatisfying comfort zone will naturally color your mood, but a significant degree of depression may keep you stuck in that dissatisfaction for far too long. If depression is part of what keeps you slumped on that dead horse, you'll need help to get off. Summon the energy to reach out, if only a bit—the possibility of support is all around you.

Certainly depression is not the only black hole into which your energy might mysteriously disappear. Any circumstance that saps your energy—three kids under five, a grindstone job, daily contact with a toxic friend, serious debt, or, like Lydia, tedious work with no one to love—might suppress desire along with it. Oh, you will have fantasies of winning the lottery, or retiring to a beach, or meeting the perfect man. But specific motivating visions of a life beyond your comfort zone are likely to be suppressed as you slog your way through your burdens.

Circumstances sap our juice for living, but for some that faith and life fuel seems to have been depleted early on through an excruciating range of punishing early experiences. Sufferers point, accurately, to harsh parents, favored siblings, school bullies, early rejections, and other disorders of love to account for their unfaltering prediction that they will receive no better, probably deserve no better, and would certainly be fools to desire better. Psychologist Sidney Simon observed that the belief "I don't deserve better" is the number one obstacle to change. Cling to this belief and it's a safe bet that you will ride a dead horse forever. After all, you know where it's going.

The desires we suppress—whether through depression or exhaustion, or in defense of our own painful vulnerabilities—are never perfectly extinguished. Inner whispers float over even our high walls, summoned by some catalyst. A friend appreciates your well-told anecdote and you remember suddenly that you want to write. Your husband unexpectedly calls to apologize and months of angry apathy melt into an image of loving possibility. The neighbor sells his house and your own niggling urge to move clicks into full focus. Perhaps the forgotten piece of a nighttime dream stalks you for half a day until it crystallizes into a vision of desire.

How can you turn the volume up on those whispers? You will need to have completed step one, of course, eliminating your distractions and facing what hurts. You will likely need treatment for your depression, support to ease your exhaustion, and intense cognitive work if your belief that you don't deserve better squashes desire before it can blossom. If you feel, though, that you have sufficient psychological energy to act, and enough optimism to feel entitled to ordinary rewards, then how do you unearth desire?

Go to step seven: Take Action.

The fact is, many people take a circuitous path to discover desire. If desire doesn't find you, then you must set off to search for it, and that journey is particularly difficult because of its uncertain destination. The point, however, is to just get yourself out on the road.

Especially if you are exiting a comfort zone because time's up—retiring from a career, losing your full-time parent position because your kids have outgrown you, stepping down from an organization you ran or away from an issue you championed—you may not necessarily be swept with a fresh hunger. Knowing it is time to let go is not the same as knowing where you want to go next. How, then, do you resuscitate desire?

When you are leaving an old platform with no sure passion driving you to the new, steer by three principles:

- *Find some creative expression.* It does not matter what form that creativity takes. Paint, throw pots, glue ceramics, keep a journal, write a children's book, join a poetry group. Perfect your pasta sauce, plan and plant a garden. Play an instrument, find a choir, join a community theater, decorate a dollhouse. Imagine how long this list could be, and neither its specific contents nor the quality of what you produce is crucial to your result. All that matters is that you are engaged in some creative process on a regular, preferably daily, basis. *Suppressed desire lives in your unconscious and the creative process is one of the keys to that kingdom.* Just find a niche where you can participate with pleasure and see what desires float to the top.

- *Serve others.* Sometimes you are standing too close to see yourself clearly. Find your own heart's desire by looking away for a while, toward something more meaningful than yourself. Search your community for a way to be of use. Your contribution does not have to be major, nor does the need you fill have to represent your true calling. Just help out with someone or something beyond yourself and your own family. Your involvement may spark you in unexpected ways. If not, at least you contributed something of value somewhere.

- *Stretch.* Beyond the principles of creativity and service, you can hunt the elusive quarry of desire in all sorts of roundabout ways since desire hides in unexpected haystacks. Some people try bombarding themselves with new choices, and if you can muster the energy for it, the result might be powerful. Even if it's not, the hunt will keep you amused.

The idea is to surprise yourself. Do the thing you always swore you wouldn't. Approve of something you've stood firmly against simply because it's an old, worn soapbox. Switch political parties and see how the other half thinks. Find yourself agreeing with the enemy, for a moment at least.

Shave your head. Eat reindeer. Gallop. Foster parent a child. Give a speech. Donate bone marrow. Sell your place and move to the beach. Pose nude. Kiss someone new. None of this is easy. All of it is accessible. It's just at the rim of your comfort zone. Once you cross that boundary, who knows where that tightrope might lead.

Other people, either more realistic or less energetic, take a modified approach to this same strategy. They take a tap dance class, learn to cook or ski or Rollerblade or to master their computer, and so open themselves to all the people who participate in these new worlds. They try interior design or bonsai or butterfly farming because they once wanted to, though these days they may hardly remember why. They resurrect childhood interests, especially those lost along the way. They sit down again at the piano, strap on the old tutu, dig out the fly-fishing rods and go forward by going back. Force yourself through these strange paces and it's very probable that desire and focus will find you.

Exercise, of course. It's the fountain of youth, health, and a new attitude. Meditate, too. It makes you brave because it shrinks your moment to this one and that's one you know you can handle. Talk to strangers. That will make fewer of them and the world won't be as scary. And for God's sake, get a change of scenery. Leave home. Not just your physical home, but your social one, too. Yes, you'll have to force yourself, but hey, that's the fight.

Tend individual sparks in small ways. Envision the marathon though you can only manage twenty-minute jogs. Carve time for your monthly book club, though there is no time to finish your play. Establish a window box while entertaining thoughts of a community garden. Tending small flames of desire is like leaving yourself a trail of bread crumbs out of your comfortable forest.

Karin does not have the problem of trying to fan a flicker of interest. Her desire is neither suppressed nor frustrated. On the contrary, it's flaming out of control, conflicted, ambivalent, and pulling her by the heart in so many contradictory directions that she ends up suffering in place.

Karin and I are drowning in a sea of maybes that undermine every motivating vision she tests. Maybe her feelings for Bob would somehow disappear; maybe she could turn back the clock to the days when she was more certain she wanted to marry Marshall. Maybe when I had fixed her and she wasn't such a whack job, she could love Marshall the way he deserved to be loved. Maybe breaking up with Marshall was the right decision, but maybe she'd regret it for the rest of her life.

Karin is similarly ambivalent about saying no to sex with Bob. True, she is offended when he calls her into the office only to toss her over a desk. It lacks . . . warmth. Still, she feels uncomfortable protesting at this point, as if she'd be delivering an "I'm not that kind of girl" speech when she has already proven to him that she is. Maybe it's better to break up altogether? But maybe she'd be giving up true love, and for what?

In the midst of this mental morass, Karin needs to create a single positive vision in order to move forward. How? She'll have to find an open door.

Find an Open Door

Karin whines. She wants it all. She wants to be a good girl. She wants to marry Marshall and have babies. She has a hot itch that only Bob can scratch and she really doesn't want to give that up. She wants every man she meets to want her, mostly because she sees it as insurance against that man being mad at her. This may be what Karin wants most of all—that neither of these men, that no man, ever be mad at her. She just hates how that feels.

What Karin wants, what she is very clear about, is that she cannot bear the thought of hurting Marshall. He's too good, and that would make her too bad. That's how they became engaged in the first place. Marshall wanted marriage and Karin couldn't think of a good reason to say no.

Karin was fairly certain her engagement was a reasonable decision, until Bob asked her for drinks one night and drinks led to the backseat of his car parked in an empty Wal-Mart lot. The adolescent outrageousness of that first sexual encounter, the perfect frenzy of it, hooked Karin. Bob's ongoing penchant for teenage groping, like his insistence on the office quickie with a secretary buzzing calls through for added spice, has proved to be less and less satisfying. Still, Karin is even less comfortable saying no to Bob than to Marshall, so she accommodates.

A theme emerges in our conversations. Karin, competitive, tomboyish Karin, submerges herself rather than hurt a man. She hides and disguises, shapes her behavior to please, too anxious to say even a small "no." How can Karin create a vision when she is not allowed to give voice to her own desires? She needs some kind of opening.

An open door is a chink in your armor. It is the vision of an appealing half step, one that puts you nearer the electric fence of anxiety but does not throw you totally up against it.

Interestingly, that door often opens inward. If you are stuck at step two and can't envision a positive outcome, look inside. Think of some trait or inhibition that has stood in your way; consider some strength you have always wanted to develop. Then picture yourself moving out of your psychological comfort zone by adding this growth to your repertoire.

For example, do you want more credit for your accomplishments but hesitate to claim it for fear of appearing to brag? Then force yourself to practice tooting your own horn, until you get more comfortable with the resulting attention. Are you overburdened because delegating means things might not be done exactly your way? Then grit your teeth and let go of control; you'll get comfortable with the passenger seat over time. Whichever skill you are working toward, new responses to old situations will put you on new ground.

Desire motivates development; development nurtures new desire. Expand your comfort zone through either portal.

Karin's open door would be to practice a simple, honest "no." No matter where Karin's current dilemma comes to rest, she will benefit from nibbling away at her discomfort with this behavior. Whether she stays in this triangle or creates a new one next year, marries Marshall or enjoys hot sex in the back of fine automobiles for a very long time to come, Karin needs the strength, the skill, and the habit of saying no when no is what she means to say.

You don't have to know where an open door is leading in order to walk through one. You just have to know that you, like Karin, can't lose anything by taking this step. Karin could only gain by following more of her own desires when it came to men.

Whether an improved ability to say no to men would help her decide more clearly between Marshall and Bob remained to be seen. But it surely couldn't hurt.

In the end I was surprised at just how much focusing emphatically on that one goal propelled Karin forward. For one thing, it moved her obsessive attention away from Marshall, Bob, guilt, and blame. Now she was reframing a personal trait, appreciating a weakness, if you will. The Karin who couldn't bear to hurt Marshall was proud of her sacrifice. In her eyes it made her a loving woman. But the Karin who was unable to say no was suddenly a weaker, less respectable Karin. That Karin needed a little work and this Karin, competitive, goal-oriented, and hardworking, was willing to put the effort in.

Karin and I worked on developing a hierarchy of situations where she could picture herself saying no to a man. These ran from least difficult (turning down her brother's request to do his laundry) to most difficult (picturing herself telling Bob to stop calling her). Creating this hierarchy was tough, because Karin was herself so uncertain of when and where she *wanted* to say no.

She agreed that she would look for opportunities to practice. I liked this plan because it had a double payoff. Practicing anxiety-producing behavior automatically meant Karin was stretching the limits of her current comfort zone. She was also, in effect, excavating and strengthening her awareness of desire. She has to stop and ask herself, "What do I really want to do here?" That simple pause for thought puts Karin in touch with herself in a way she has ignored for too long. In the guise of looking for situations in which to say no, Karin is practicing listening and knowing herself.

It worked, because Karin did. I often collaborate with patients to develop simple exercises, but much of the time they fail to complete the task. A crisis comes up, they grow distracted, the exercise was too threatening or too easy or too wide of the mark, or the person is too mired in avoidance to take on a specific task. Karin, on the other hand, was willing.

She looked for opportunities to assert herself against male will and then talked about how anxious it made her to express herself. Sometimes, as when Marshall wanted her to vacation with his family, she blurted out her feelings before she could scare herself into keeping silent. Sometimes, as when Bob wanted her to take a business trip with him but stay stashed in their hotel room to protect his marriage, we practiced for several sessions before she could speak her piece.

For several months, we focused weekly on understanding what Karin did and did not wish to do, how she communicated those decisions and how she could withstand the disappointment or anger those decisions sometimes engendered. Karin practiced and she got better.

Saying no was an open door that put one foot firmly outside Karin's comfort zone. It helped her to see that she has a far greater degree of control over her personal life than she has been willing to exercise. With focused effort and considerable practice, Karin got better at knowing what she wanted and braver about asking for it.

Part of her was headed out the door, but part was still stuck. Karin's practice in decision making and self-expression concerned smaller, more specific personal situations. She still lingered in a confused agony over the big life crossroads.

She will still have to choose between Marshall and Bob. Surely her affair is a certain sign that marriage to Marshall is all wrong? But how can she know that, know for sure? Maybe this is just a bad patch in a potentially great relationship, an indication of her own fear of commitment. How can she judge whether her passion for Bob signals true love or the simple high of bad behavior? How can she take action without knowing for certain?

How can any of us risk change when we still wonder if things will get better if only we stay where we are for a little while longer? In other words, how do any of us know, actually know, that our particular horse is dead?

CHAPTER 5

HOW DO YOU KNOW
IF THE HORSE IS DEAD?

The mathematics of self-directed change is simple: First, pay attention to your own pain. Second, believe there is something better out there for you. Add discomfort to desire and you ought to get movement.

You don't, of course. Not direct, unopposed movement, that is. What you'll experience instead are your own internal urges toward change as they come up against all the fears and attachments that hold you in place. Sneaking past your own obstacles is the subject of the rest of this book.

At some point you will mount a full frontal assault on your doubt and fear, but in the early stages it's more likely that doubt and fear will initiate the assaults on you. You will writhe, agonize, churn with questions. Sure, you feel pain, sadness, frustration, but isn't that all part of adult life? Yes, this relationship is hurtful and hard, but haven't you been warned that the best ones are work? True, this lover is close in a way your wife has never been, but does that mean you abandon a marriage and kids? And the job that's a misery still pays the rent, and what makes you think it will be less miserable elsewhere?

As clearly as your unhappiness may call out to you, you will probably still wonder whether it's yelling "Time to move on" or sending a signal to endure and try harder. As powerful as the grip of some new passion is, you will still be reluctant to give up everything you have for the sake of its satisfaction. Apprehension will join forces with your conscience and your common sense. Together they will shriek in an arresting chorus: *How do I know if the horse is dead?*

How do you know if the marriage is over, or should be? How do you know when to fire the inept employee? How do you recognize the promotion's not coming and it's time to look outside the company? What finally tells you you'll never sell the novel or make a living as a working actress and you must create another vision of happiness? How do you know, when a lover asks for more time, how much time to give? When your partner says he'll stop drinking or spending or flirting, when must you accept that he won't?

How can any of us know, for sure, that the comfort zone in which we have nestled will absolutely, positively not yield enough of what we want or need at some time in the future?

The painful answer is this: In one sense you may know, but in another you will never know for sure. Inevitably you will have to decide. That decision is the killer. In the end, your horse isn't dead until you get off it—even if it's only walking you around in circles.

A Sense of What You Know

What's the decision facing you? Are you wondering if you should put more money into the business or close it? Are you clinging to your profession while part of you believes you should be home full-time with the kids? Or are you home with the kids but in need of more income and too scared to test yourself in the marketplace? Do you hesitate at the idea of going into your own practice, or painting full-time, or moving in with someone, uncertain whether to move ahead?

Whichever your question, there's a good chance you already know the answer.

It may not be the "right" answer; it is often an uncomfortable or difficult answer, but many people are able to tap into an internal voice, guiding them to a true answer. Ask your own version of the question: How do I know if my particular horse is dead? If you turn a vigilant ear to that inner voice, you may discover that, intuitively, you simply *know*.

Intuition, "the unconscious summing up of knowledge," as psychoanalyst Otto Fenichel elegantly defined it, is available to light the way out of your comfort zone. But you will need to find your own path to that intuitive voice. There are a number of inner-journey techniques that I and others can offer to guide you, but I've never found a one-size-fits-all version. My personal favorite is described in Adelaide Bry's book *Visualization*, but I find that if I recommend that or some other resource to ten people, only one or two ever follow up. Such indifference strengthens my conviction that active seeking is necessary to enhance the value of any technique.

On the other hand, when you are stuck in a comfort zone, a good kick in the path never hurts. In that spirit, here's a simple turning-inward technique to try. First, read the next several paragraphs through, then go back and try the exercise.

Slowly take four deep breaths in through your nose, then exhale loudly through your mouth. Again. Now, close your eyes and try it—four breaths in through the nose, one out through the mouth. When you've finished three cycles of this relaxation breathing, keep your eyes closed, breathe normally, focus on the backs of your eyelids, and think about your problem. Ask yourself: *What do I need to do next? Is now the time I need to do it?* Pay attention to the thoughts and especially to the visual images that come to mind. Maybe you'll discover an answer you hadn't realized you knew.

There is an important second step to any of these inner dialogues. Once you get an answer to your question, however vague, write that answer down. Your discovery may be difficult news. The natural anesthetics of the psyche will seek to erase your discomfort. Writing is a way of holding on to what you know against the inner tides of avoidance, denial, fantasy, and blame that are working to wash away your intuition.

This exercise is one of many ways to pay attention to what you already know. Any relaxation exercise that you prefer can substitute for the breathing I described. Sitting in silence, closing your eyes, and looking inward is a time-honored technique of self-discovery, but journal writing, beach walking, meditation, or prayer might all give you access to your own opinion about your necessary next step.

Remember Lydia, who daydreamed about boyfriends and babies but lived a paperwork life? Lydia and I worked hard to dig past her fantasy and denial so she could face what hurt. When we did, though, we found a lonely, uncertain woman. Lydia's life vision was powerful and true. She saw herself in that messy, happy country house full of love. Ah, but could she, actually *should* she, try to create that home on her own?

To choose single parenthood seemed, well, both horrifying and thrilling. Was it possible? Was it moral? Was it wise? Now? Or ever? Only Lydia could answer these questions, but how could she come to know her true answers?

Lydia found her clearest access to self-knowledge at her church, where she conducted an ongoing debate with God regarding his plans for her and her right to make plans for herself. "I used to pray and get angry, asking God why he made me such a loving person if he wouldn't send me anyone to love. I would say, 'This lonely life can't be what you had in mind for me.'

"I asked over and over and finally I started to answer the questions in my own head. 'I'm sad' and 'I'm angry' became 'God, you gave me so much love to give. Who will I give it to?' Then I'd get the image of a baby, a little baby, and the energizing mantra of my childhood would pop into my head: 'God helps those who help themselves.' I knew."

Have your own discussion with your God. Maybe you'll know, too.

It's one thing to know a personal truth through whatever technique works. It's quite another to get yourself to pay attention to what you know. I have heard men and women explain exactly what was wrong with a partner from the first date—wrong religion, wrong body type, insufficient ambition, excess of gold jewelry, for example. Yet some pursued long romantic relationships with these very same partners. These men and women invested huge chunks of time in attachments that were tethered to an anchor from the outset. They chose to ignore what they knew.

I've worked with patients who have told me, after a job interview, that the work seemed tedious yet took the job, burrowed in, and struggled with the question of how to move on. I've seen patients go off to graduate school at the urging of well-intentioned families and flounder miserably because they knew from the start they had no interest in the program.

When people know at the outset that their paths lead nowhere, why take them anyway?

Because it's easy, because it's comfortable, because easy and comfortable leave us insulated from pain, fear, and anxiety. Because once you give in to easy and comfortable, it's as if you are in the grip of a giant suction force pulling you back to familiar turf, regardless of what you know to the contrary. Because, as we've discussed, it's simpler to erase your knowing—with fantasy, avoidance, denial, or blame—than to pay attention to painful truths.

In the struggle to get past these barriers, though, you may have separate moments of perfect clarity, moments when you acknowledge that the only way to improve your situation is to change it. You simply know—in your gut or your heart or wherever it is your intuition shouts your name. These intuitive assessments— drawn from too many subtle variables for you to be completely conscious of them—result in a compelling emotional truth.

In such moments, you *know* whether this friendship, this job, this partnership, this love affair, this project is dead in the water. Then, after you know, you'll look at it from another angle and doubt yourself again.

Karin has many such moments of clarity when she talks at length about why she should, why she *must*, end her relationship with her married lover. It needs to end, she says, whether she marries her fiancé or not, because she recognizes that its best days are past. Instead of being thrilled, she's anxious around Bob; instead of feeling special, she's feeling guilty; instead of feeling secure, she's feeling as if her job might be at risk. Karin reads her feelings like tea leaves and she knows her next step.

Karin's realistic view of her future with Bob is unusual enough to mention. Unlike so many people in affairs with married partners, Karin does not diminish her pain with the fantasy of marriage. She is not dreaming of the day when Dr. Bob will leave his wife, though he sometimes hints to her that he might.

Other women or men, fiercely in love with their married partners, have a far more difficult time "knowing" that the relationship will never move forward. They dangle helplessly on promises of imminent separations and future marriage plans. Isn't that worth waiting for, they ask? After all, some lovers end up together in these circumstances. Not very often, but often enough to wait and see.

Occasionally, these promises of a future are only the most callous of manipulations, lies told by sexually gratified partners who are interested in being continuously serviced. As several have explained to me over the years with comfortable self-justification, "I have to tell her I'm leaving my wife. She'd probably stop seeing me if I didn't."

On the other hand, these promises are often sincere, made by loving men and women trying to get the courage to abandon the security of their own stale comfort zones. But they are promises made that may or may not be fulfilled. How can you know the difference? Who knows how long is long enough to wait for a married lover to make the leap? You don't know. You decide.

Clearly, knowing is not enough. Even if, like Karin, you know absolutely what you should do, you will still have to decide whether to do it. If, like Lydia, you know what steps you could take, you still have to weigh the risks of taking them.

And quite frankly, you may look inside and be more like Ryan or Jack, who discovered they were as profoundly ambivalent when they looked inward as from any other view. In fact, many of us retreat from the world's din, focus on a question, and discover an inner voice that sounds like a Florida election, full of hanging chads and if onlys, our intuition dependent on all the different ways its vote might be counted.

Is your horse dead? Are you stuck in a comfort trap? Whether you know the answer or not, you will still have to decide. That decision is nothing more or less than a bet.

Placing Your Bet

The brilliant psychiatrist Peter Kramer once considered the question *Should You Leave?* from every conceivable angle. His answer was exactly what you'd suspect: It depends.

It depends on who you are and what you value. It depends on how you ask the question and in what emotional state you consider the possibilities. It depends on whom you consult for your answer and how you take in what they say. But ultimately, it depends on you and what you decide.

Don't you hate that? I once conceived a plan to exchange life decisions with a friend. In theory, I would call this person— presumably clever and with my best interests at heart—and present a dilemma. Should I have a second child, is it time to buy an office building for my practice, should I confront my father or leave well enough alone? Then I would simply act on whatever my adviser decided, thereby saving myself untold hours of dithering. I would of course be available to my friend, to make some similarly momentous life decision should the occasion arise. I thought this was an excellent scheme, but I could never quite find that special person to whom I would turn over my life. I am, however, still looking.

My patients are certainly still looking and they naturally look to me as one possibility. They request advice indirectly, because it is generally understood that psychotherapists are not permitted, by union regulations, to give advice. I recognize how pervasive this rumor is by the number of people who say to me, "I know you aren't allowed to give advice, but . . ."

The fact is, I have nothing against giving advice if I think it would spare a person pain and point him or her in a productive direction. The problem is that I usually don't know what to advise, and when I do, people rarely listen anyway. Much as we dislike the weight of decisions, we hate even more to have our lives decided for us.

So we retain our power to decide and then we sometimes stagger under the weight of that power:

Consider Ramon, who will need to beg and borrow from his family to keep his restaurant open through the current economic slowdown. His wife shudders at the prospect of deeper dependence on her in-laws. His siblings are divided about whether Ramon is entitled to such support. His business advisers can't predict the future, and Ramon's entire sense of self is entangled with the continued success of this restaurant. He can't picture any other life.

What about Hope, who accidentally falls in love with her neighbor though she is in the middle of a pleasant marriage with only ordinary unhappiness. Hope knows what her marriage is, says it does not "entitle" her to leave. Her own mother advises her that if she divorces and remarries, "You're trading one pile of shit for another." That's true, she thinks, but desire is drawing her to the tightrope.

Think of Barbara, seventy-one, whose husband is insisting on retiring to Florida while Barbara is considering having a second face-lift and opening a thrift shop. The family says she is fighting her future. Barbara insists she is welcoming it. Her marriage may split if Barbara pursues her course. Which is the dead horse?

I don't know. I don't know whether Ryan should cut loose from his family or vie for leadership within it; whether Lydia should strike out on her own for a child or make more realistic efforts to find a partner; whether Ramon should reinvest in his business or Hope should reinvest in her marriage; whether Barbara's new life plan represents a burst of independent courage or a flood of fears about aging. I do know, at least, that Karin ought to dump Bob, but what the hell, she knows that, too.

I don't know for sure what any of them should do, and neither do they. Each of these people is required, in effect, to place a bet on his or her life. Let the chips ride where they are or move them somewhere new, where the odds are more promising or the play more thrilling. However much the odds improve, even the decision to stay is still a bet.

The people we've talked about so far—like Jack deciding between a beloved fantasy and a flawed woman; Karin, with her choice of lovers; Ryan working for and against himself; or Lydia, agonizing over an unorthodox parenthood—all have one thing in common. Each is, at least, placing the bet on him- or herself. It's even trickier to decide to leave a comfort zone when the bet you are placing is on someone else.

If you've been waiting in your comfort zone for something essential to your satisfaction, how do you know when you've waited long enough? Especially if that vital something has been promised, you might hang on the hook of that expectation indefinitely—until you realize that only you can pronounce the horse dead. But how long do you wait to make that pronouncement?

If, for example, you are waiting for someone to change—to control his nasty temper, to lose weight, to be more organized, honest, or responsible—and that person fervently agrees to the change, wants it perhaps even more than you do, how many years do you put up a fight before you exit the battlefield?

When do you call creative aspirations mere escapist daydreams? At the first real-life failure? At the fortieth? How do you distinguish between perseverance and pigheadedness?

If the promotion does not materialize, the promised staffing change is never forthcoming, the training is always postponed, when do you decide to make a professional change?

When you are promised a future, whether professional or personal, but there is no ironclad guarantee that anyone will deliver on this promise, when do you walk away from hope?

Each of these situations is an example of an emotional hook on which a life might dangle for an indefinite period of time. Such hooks are ripely baited—with expectations of money, love, success, security, peace of mind, or some other richly desired goal. Each hook keeps its victim snagged to a spot, digging in deeper and deeper with every ounce of effort put toward the goal.

Think of a stuck tire, spinning in a snowbank. Give the car gas and the tire will plow deeper into the hole, but it will not necessarily go forward. Like that tire, all the effort you put forth, trying to fulfill your frustrated hopes, may dig you even more deeply into an unsatisfying comfort zone. After all, look at what you've invested. The world around you is shouting "This is going nowhere," but continuing to spin in place makes you less anxious than giving up.

In these situations, full of promise but short on payoff, it's very tough to establish objective guidelines for letting go. Particularly when your comfort zone centers around a relationship, even the obvious signals—if someone is reviling you, hitting you, stealing from you, or vomiting on his own shoes and leaving it for you to clean up—have the occasional exceptions. Besides, it's hard to turn your back on crumbs if you are desperately hungry.

The undertow of a comfort zone shared by two people can be overwhelming. Nothing is simple in the ties between two people. There are crucial needs served in a bad relationship, just as there are essential longings that go unfulfilled in a good one. Always it is possible to make lists of pros and cons, to weigh and measure decisions of the heart. But the lists are little more than a touching pantomime of objectivity.

So are the clear arguments you make, explaining *why* you are entitled to have whatever it is your partner withholds, why it is only fair, only reasonable, in both of your best interests that your partner (or your sister, your child, or your friend, for that matter) make the changes you want. Your arguments will be persuasive. They will be right. Even your partner may agree with them. Those rational arguments rarely make a bit of difference.

Most of what you are waiting for in a relationship will not come if it hasn't already, and you will live without it. You have already demonstrated that you can do so, because, for however long you've been waiting, you have. The absence of some *key* satisfactions, though, make even that comfort zone too bleak to endure. You, knowing yourself, will decide which elements are key.

Ryan's wife can live with her husband smoking pot every

night. She doesn't like it, and nags him to stop, but she lives with it. Maybe for you that would be the deal breaker. Jane needs the ring, needs the marriage, needs the commitment, and so she is seriously evaluating whether it is time to stop waiting. Another woman—perhaps one who already has her children or doesn't want a child, perhaps a financially independent woman who doesn't want to risk her assets—wouldn't consider Jack's reluctance to marry quite so serious, because she can feel satisfied and secure without it.

If you are waiting for someone to make a key change and you are wondering how long to wait, here is the bottom line: You will cut yourself loose from the emotional hook when you decide that, regardless of the sweet comforts of hope, you are quite simply done dangling. That's when you know you've waited long enough. You'll move your happiness chips off this other person and place the bet on yourself.

By contrast to the complex uncertainty of personal relationships, objective signals that you've hit a professional blank wall are generally easier to identify. But the hooks—the next round of promotions, seasonal bonuses, retirement packages, promises for future projects, or changes in administration—may pin you just as firmly as a faulty relationship does. In both instances you are secure but unsatisfied where you are. Yet satisfaction has been promised, in some indeterminate future. You are held in place, waiting.

At work, though, impersonal assessment can help you evaluate your real possibilities for promotion; company or professional pay scales can predict your earning potential, and personnel reviews provide at least some reflection of your status. Avoidance, denial, and fantasy are probably your biggest obstacles to clear decision making. The signs of corporate favor, the earning ceilings in a company, the promotion and growth patterns of a job, are often flashing all around. We sometimes don't want to force ourselves to see.

The real problem, though, with recognizing work as a comfort trap generally is not the unfulfilled hope of advancement but the lulling numbness of familiarity. Many jobs offer at least the illusion of indefinite security, with clear rewards and predictable workload. We know the people, we know the place, we know the parking lot. It's a brain groove—five days a week, move through these tasks, decide between the tuna and the burger for lunch, distract yourself with enough office intrigue to make the day interesting, drive home. Push a little in the busy times, space out a little when you can, prefer the busy times actually and move on to the next day.

What's wrong with this picture? Absolutely nothing, as long as, in addition to the lulling sense of security, you also have a tolerable degree of personal satisfaction delivered with your tuna. Personal satisfaction may take many forms—intellectual stimulation, skill development, a sense of higher purpose, the value of team membership, pride in product, or sheer daily fun. All these satisfactions have one common element. They are *intrinsic* satisfactions, gratifications from the job itself, rather than extrinsic satisfactions, namely the pay and perks you receive for doing the job.

We work for the money, first and foremost. Your relative satisfaction with your pay and perks is obviously a requirement for professional well-being. But it's not enough, and no amount of money will make it enough, if the job itself is deadly. All the money and perks will do is keep you there too long because they are difficult to relinquish. Ryan is in exactly this dilemma, hand-cuffed to a lucrative situation that so far affords him none of the pleasures that work has to offer.

Joseph Campbell famously guided us to "follow your bliss," exhilarating advice that makes those of us who followed our mortgages hang our heads a little. When I talk about intrinsic sat-isfactions I am not pushing for anything quite so exalted as bliss. (Bliss would be good, though.) It's just simple fact that if your work no longer offers you much to learn, much to laugh about, much to take pride in or pleasure from, then it's not a very satisfy-ing ride.

Odds are you are there because it's a comfort zone, because it's easy, because it pays the bills. If you have other sources of plea-sure and pride, opportunities to learn and accomplish in some arena other than work (your kids, your golf game, your volunteer work, your music) and you need the secure job to pay the bills, then so be it. But check that you aren't merely rationalizing away your own inertia. Work takes up the best hours of the day. Are there really enough left over for you to get satisfaction from those other avenues?

Love and work, the two great life endeavors, can stagnate un-til you make an active decision to change them. Those decisions are rarely clear, never easy, and usually not wholehearted. But difficult, murky, and even halfhearted decisions are still powerful enough to get your life moving again, and that's all you need.

"Will this boss eventually get fired, or do I have to leave be-fore I kill him?"

"It's my third year of medical school and it's not getting better. But how do I walk away when I have so much invested?"

"I built this charity from the ground up. Now new people want me to step back and let them run it. I don't want to, but maybe it's time?"

"Is this all there is?" No. It's not.

Increasing Your Odds

How do you know when the horse is dead? When you don't know for sure, you place your bet. But you can increase the odds in your own favor. Here's what to keep in mind as you make that decision.

First, there is usually no one best choice. There are only choices and their consequences. Some of those consequences will be negative, because if there were one perfect choice you'd have no problem at all.

The simple fact that *no matter what you decide, there will be some negative consequence to that decision* should be perfectly obvious. Nevertheless, people have a hard time wrapping their minds around it.

Jack wrestles mentally with marriage, sees what he doesn't like about it, backs off and turns against Jane, feels pain and embraces the idea of Jane, and begins again to wrestle with marriage. But he won't make much progress until he accepts the fact that no matter which path he chooses, some aspect of his choice will hurt. There's just no getting around that when a decision challenges your comfort zone. If you act, something makes you anxious; if you stay put, something is lost.

Some consequences are subtle and unexpected. For example, there may be serious strain in Ramon's relationship with his siblings if he borrows family money to save his business, even if the business is successful. Their parents did not rescue other children in trying financial circumstances. What makes Ramon more deserving? Ramon needs to consider those family consequences in his decision making, even if he resents the injustice of it.

Hope is temporarily flattened by the idea that it will cost her if she leaves her marriage and it will cost her if she stays. Barbara, at seventy-one, is more at peace with those costs. As she reminds me, there's no free lunch.

So, swallow the hard truth that there is no one right choice and then go one step further. Recognize that you will make the best choice you can, given who you are and what your circumstances are *at this moment in your life*. Will you regret it later? Maybe, if you are the sort who is given to regret. But that future review changes nothing. The choice is on today's table, regarding today's comfort zone. Everything you are to this point is all you can bring to your decision. Believe me, it will be enough.

Armed with the understanding that

- There is no one right choice,
- Whatever you choose will involve some loss, some pain, or some difficulty *even if you choose to stay exactly where you are,*
- You can only make the decision you are capable of today, because today is when the question is called,

you can now judiciously consider the question How do I decide if the horse is dead?

Your goal, when you are making the difficult decision, is to *think deeply* and then *act directly*.

Thinking deeply means two things. First, it means looking

back at your life to understand your current decision in a wider context. (The next chapter discusses that look back in detail.) Second, deep reflection requires a look into the future, actively envisioning the short- and long-term consequences of whatever decision is under consideration.

Acting directly means keeping a steady balance, resisting both the temptation to act impulsively and the urge to avoid any action at all, disappearing instead into blame, fantasy, or denial. Between your urge to avoid and your impulse to act without thinking is the evenhanded execution of a step in the right direction.

And how do you decide which direction to bet on? The following signposts might help.

Check for a Pulse

Squint at your comfort zone. Any signs of life? Whether it is a job, a business, a marriage, a friendship, or a lifestyle that you are evaluating, the vital signs are similar. Is there emotional zest, sexual pleasure, companionship, life support, personal satisfaction, intellectual challenge, or a sense of future potential? Few situations offer all these rewards (and if you are in one, for God's sake, stay there). If your situation offers little or none of these rewards, it's dead, plain and simple.

James, married twenty-six years to a woman who no longer wants a sexual relationship, paused for a long time over this question as he considered his marriage. Finally he summed up his and every person's agony when he considers leaving a marriage that still has signs of life, however faint. "Just because it's not enough," he said, "doesn't mean it's nothing."

Like James, only you can decide, as you look at your familiar circumstances, if the spark of warmth, the history of better days, the sheer momentum of your comfort zone is life enough to sustain your future.

Look Behind Your Back

Sometimes our unconscious makes decisions that we are unable to acknowledge consciously. That's how we manage to get fired from jobs we didn't have the gumption to leave. That's how the hot e-mail flirtation we thought we'd deleted ends up being seen by a spouse. Take a careful look at the choices you've made. You may discover that you have left yourself secret messages regarding your decision.

Karin certainly sent unconscious hints to Marshall, half hoping he'd see the bad Karin and so leave her with a lighter heart. But Marshall studiously looked away.

Ryan, too, had a disconnect between his stated intentions and his behavior. Consciously, Ryan only bad-mouthed the business, but we noticed that he never missed a family dinner, called in from vacations, and insinuated himself into every company issue. It began to look to me as if under his bad-boy rebellion was a company president waiting to break out. But could he let go of his comfortable identity in order to make the leap?

The point is that useful information for your difficult decisions may come as much from what you do as from what you think or feel. Take a careful look around.

Take Your Temperature

After long months of ambivalence, Ramon finally decided to close his restaurant and take a job as an executive chef. Neither economic indicators, marital pressures, nor the halfhearted support of his siblings changed his mind. Instead, he finally stopped to pay attention to his own unhappiness. "Here's what I learned," he told me. "If the path you are on causes you constant pain, *it's the wrong path.*"

How much pain are you experiencing and what does that pain produce? Emotional pain can be productive, signaling that you are tackling something difficult, or it can be merely tormenting. For example, if Karin confronts Bob, his blast of anger will definitely hurt, but she'll discover she's still standing when it passes. That's pain in the service of progress. But the guilty wounds inflicted when she lies or acquiesces gain her nothing.

Is your pain chronic or intermittent? Intermittent pain is unavoidable unless you bury yourself so deep in a comfort zone that you don't feel much of anything at all. It is the ouch of testing your limits, of facing a risk, of enduring disappointment and climbing out of failure. Chronic emotional pain, though, is the bellwether of a bad relationship or soul-killing work. Act accordingly.

Measure Your Degree of Control

Your time on an emotional hook should depend on how much you can do to make things better. Some desired outcomes, like quitting smoking, for example, are entirely under your control. Others, like getting your husband to quit smoking, are not one iota under your control. The rest of what we wait and hope for is somewhere in between. How much of what you are waiting for is under your own management?

Ramon could control the quality of his restaurant but he cannot control the economy that determines how often people go out to dinner. James can approach his wife for sex more insistently or more persuasively, but he cannot control her response. Both of them can take steps to get what they want, but they cannot entirely control the outcome. They need to adjust their time in the comfort zone in light of this limitation.

Most emotional hooks are baited with someone else's promises. That puts their fulfillment out of your control. The true purpose of waiting around is not so much to get what you want as it is to learn if you can live without it. Once you have that answer, the waiting period is over, one way or the other. You know what satisfactions this comfort zone will or will not offer. Decide on that basis.

Have You Tried Everything?

When Winston Churchill advised us to "never, never, never, never, never, never, never, never give up," he was not referring to lending money yet again to your drug-addicted brother in the hope that he will clean up his act. Perseverance is a glorious strength—to the degree that your goal is under your control. If you are hanging on an emotional hook, there is only so much you can do to push, prod, lure, seduce, argue, convince, or manipulate your way into getting what you are waiting for. When you've done it all, and you keep on going, you risk working against yourself.

It's a bell-shaped curve. A little nagging has maximum impact if it's going to have any impact at all. After a certain point (if you are wondering where that point is, I would bet you are already past it) your urging has a negative impact. Now you are simply in a power struggle. Past this point, the harder you push the chubby spouse to diet, or the lazy kid to exercise more, or the reluctant woman to have sex, or the bachelor to produce the ring, the more the other person will push back to stay comfortable.

You've shifted the onus of change from his or her shoulders onto your own. You push for change. He pushes to remain the same. Stalemate.

At this point, your only option is to give up the struggle and see what happens. Just drop the ball. Think of yourself as a Navy SEAL forced into radio silence to protect a covert operation. Stop pushing and see what happens.

One of two things will result. Free of the power struggle that was slowing things down, your partner will either step forward and deliver . . . or not. Either way, you will know that you have tried everything.

How long should you wait until you feel convinced that the results are in? Who knows? For as long as you can, or for as long as it takes for you to become convinced that whatever change you are awaiting is not going to occur. When you have tried everything and reached that stalemate, the horse is dead. Live with it or get off.

Is There Any Hard Evidence?

When you are deciding whether the horse is dead, don't just go by your gut. Look around at the data and make your most realistic assessment. If your spouse says he regrets the affair and won't make that mistake again, can you believe him? Has he changed jobs to avoid the girlfriend, sought help to change his behavior, and passed every new trust test you've thrown his way? If so, you have some data to suggest that your marriage is alive and kicking. If, on the other hand, he swears they are now just friends, but he's working with her every day and he resents your anxious inquiries, you've seriously got to question his commitment to monogamy. Not promises, but deeds and data constitute hard evidence. Pay attention to them.

Are the People You Trust Trying to Tell You Something?

These days the people you trust are worse than therapists when it comes to giving open advice. With the possible exception of your mother or your bossy older sister, many friends are so reluctant to go out on a limb they will look the other way at almost anything. Therefore, if you are hearing a chorus of advice, and it's all shouting "Get out of there," it's worth paying attention to.

Have You Considered a Compromise?

It's easy to be blinded by either/or thinking, especially when making a difficult decision. Yet the middle of the road is sometimes a path's most creative alternative. Compromise is not always easy to identify, though, when you are ricocheting between emotional poles. Barbara, for example, was reluctant to separate from her husband but equally reluctant to follow him into the retirement for which he was pressing. In the end, the three of us worked together to forge a tolerable compromise.

Barbara's husband agreed to pay for her second face-lift (and decided, to her shock, to have one himself) and Barbara opened her thrift shop in Florida so the two of them could continue to live together. It was not a perfect solution. Her husband's business support was grudging and Barbara faulted herself privately for being too weak to leave him and live on her own. Still, she took the half step she was capable of and kept the measure of security she required. When I last saw them, her husband was handling Barbara's books and was happily writing off her visit to the grandchildren by insisting she scour every junk shop on the East Coast for merchandise.

Think compromise when you are struggling over an either/or decision. Not every add-on in life requires that you give something up.

How Long Has It Been Since You've Had a Good Time?

Pain is one sign, but the absence of pleasure is also a good indicator that it's time to make yourself a little uncomfortable.

When you don't feel much of anything at all, when there is no excitement, no ambition, no energy, *something is wrong*. If this is not a response to recent loss or hard times, then it's a signal that your comfort zone is turning into an emotional tomb. Sometimes you discover that the horse that's dead is you.

To answer your own version of the question "How do I know if this horse is dead?" you may find it best to consider the previous points in a thoughtful and orderly way. Conversely, one signal might ring over and over in your consciousness.

You might make these evaluations over a period of months or in minutes. Always you will be fighting your tendency to avoid the subject, your wish to deny your own painful conclusions or to daydream about unlikely rescues.

However you go about making your decision, be on the lookout for a focusing moment, that mobilizing intersection of intuition and action that will clearly light your way.

The Focusing Moment

Change itself is such a circuitous, irregular, and inefficient process, it seems impossible to define the moment when it occurs. We are less likely to make a change than to slide, nibble, stomp, and then tippy-toe toward one.

Still, in all our ambivalence and uncertainty, there sometimes comes a crystal moment of clarity. People who have initiated constructive change in their lives are often able to identify such a moment. Asked to look back, many could promptly recall the exact instant when they knew it was time to let go:

"I was dragging my heels about selling the store. When my business partner brought his psychiatrist to a meeting so they could analyze my 'sharing problem,' I decided I didn't want to share anymore."

"I would cry on the bathroom floor nearly every night after my husband said something ugly. One night, I think I left my body and saw myself crying by the toilet. I knew I'd be spending a lot of my time next to this toilet unless I left this marriage. I called the lawyer in the morning."

"When they brought in the retirement counselors to help us make a long-term plan, I thought, 'Holy shit, I'm thirty years old and they are telling me I could die in this job.' Six months later I found myself employed as cook on a private yacht sailing the Pacific, wondering if I had overreacted."

"I thought I had been doing fine, proving I could make it on my own after my husband left me with a two-year-old and a two-month-old. My in-laws had been offering to help, but that was the last place I wanted to be. Then both my kids got chicken pox at the same time and my boss told me I had to come in to work anyway. It made me face facts. I thought, 'Wow. This is really not in the best interests of my children. I need support. Period.' I gritted my teeth and I moved."

"It had all happened already. His affair. Our confrontation. Their breakup. Endless marriage analysis. Friends' shock. Family support. Six months of drama, pain, crying, but no particular game plan. One day I was sitting at the dining room table when he came home from work and I asked, 'How was your day?' He tilted his head in a gesture I recognized too well. It meant 'Bad day. I need cheering up.' At that exact moment, I quit the marriage. I thought, 'I don't want to do the happy dance to cheer up a husband who feels bad because he broke up with his girlfriend.' "

"I had two huge professional disappointments in a row," said a senior lobbyist. "First, I was fired from a fantastic job, and then I was nearly hired at another one but it fell through. When I got the phone call that the new job was a no go, I knew, absolutely, that I had to be in business for myself. I took that second phone call as a sign."

In the last chapter we talked about "finding an open door"— that is, taking one tiny step outside your comfort zone without necessarily knowing where you are going. Karin, for example, deliberately practiced saying no to a man's request as a first step toward being strong enough to decide about Marshall and Bob. Her open door was something she worked at.

Sometimes, though, indefinable forces may offer you a strong sense of direction in the form of an insight, an intuition, or a vision. We create open doors through our own conscious efforts, but a focusing moment may feel like it was delivered, a gift of guidance from some higher source, whether inside or outside ourselves. We get a sign from the universe, a wink from God, that points the way in a dark time. Or, like Jack's moment of watching Jane care for a child on the beach, we experience an instant of new certainty surfacing through the soup of our ambivalence.

Whether from some greater power or through the power of your own careful attention, directional signs can only be read when you are looking for them. For example, a lackluster marriage may endure indefinitely. Then one evening on a business trip you enjoy a long laugh with a colleague. If you listen, that laugh may be the sound of every vague thing that has been missing at home, and may help you to leave your shroud and seek out real emotional contact—in your marriage or outside it. If you are not listening, it will only be a pleasant laugh.

The very same cue may appear and reappear until finally you open yourself to it. A woman finally leaves her bad boyfriend, saying "One Valentine's Day, I sent him a very careful card, but he went on a surprise trip without me. My shrink said, 'What are you doing with him?' which was a question I had heard over and over. Only this time for some reason I actually heard it. I saw that it was not just a question about him, but he was symbolic of all the destructive, flashy people I was involved with who were never going to have anything to give me. The shrink said, 'What you need is a solid citizen.' A year and a half later I married one, and it's been happily ever after."

The universe offers signs, focusing moments and nudges toward timely reassessments. Your friend dies of colon cancer or leaves his publishing job to open an inn, has an affair or becomes a parent—and you are given an opportunity to focus on your own progress. Miss one period, be overlooked on one round of promotions, sustain the injury that sidelines you for the season, and you have been given a strong suggestion by the universe that you should examine your choices and expand your options. The universe calls us constantly, but most often it gets a busy signal. You have to pick up.

When you do pick up, the connection can be powerful, even when it fades from the front of your consciousness. Jack squelched his warm attraction to a family with Jane almost as quickly as he felt it. But he remembered enough of it to tell me about it, and I do think the flash of feeling opened new possibilities in his imagination and therefore edged him closer to the barrier of his comfort zone.

As you may know too well, just because you have a focusing moment doesn't mean you'll make a move. Karin saw the ugly truth of her situation at an office holiday party when Bob cordially introduced her to his wife and later tried to pull Karin into his office for a quick sexual encounter. Karin surprised herself by shoving him away and leaving the party.

She felt almost instantly concerned, though, that her shove had made him mad, and she couldn't resist calling him to apologize. Her call intensified her self-loathing, while the image of Bob gleefully sneaking behind his wife's back strengthened Karin's resolve. She had always known, but now knew in a more compelling way, that this affair had to end. It was getting ugly.

If Karin's decision was so clear and firm, why couldn't she carry it out? As she suffered over why she didn't, hadn't, couldn't end it, she began to speculate on why she started the affair in the first place.

Having some sense of how you got stuck is a positive step toward extricating yourself. Resisting avoidance, interrupting blame, confronting denial, and shooting down every rescue fantasy as it showed its flower face, Karin and I began to consider the question of where she came from and what her past had to do with where she found herself today.

At this point you will want to ask yourself some of these same questions. Have you done this before? Can you identify a pattern? In other words, what was the horse you rode in on?

CHAPTER 6

LOOK BACK,
BUT DON'T STARE

B e totally clear. Change requires action. You are going to
have to do something different, and that probably means
something uncomfortable, to get to someplace new. You
can't simply think your way there or feel your way there. And you
certainly can't get there by looking behind you.

But it's a start.

Paradoxically, when action is required, stopping to think is
often the smartest way to begin. Complex choices are best guided
by some deeper appreciation of your situation, one that encom-
passes your motives, beliefs, and your covert needs. Therefore,
before you make your next move, pause to reflect on the internal
forces that have brought you to this point. Don't spend the next
few years trying to figure it out, but don't skip this step either. In
other words, look back, but don't stare.

The whole principle of looking backward—of self-examination
with a careful focus on less conscious drives—gets mixed reviews.

In the opinion of some, an analysis of one's past and inner process is, at best, nothing more than an indulgent exploration of the navel. At worst it is an excuse for irresponsible behavior or a permission slip for inaction. Plus, it's damned uncomfortable. Given these sentiments, naturally one would stonewall.

You may recall James, whose wife of twenty-six years no longer wanted any physical or sexual contact with him. Mai didn't seem to want much emotional connection either, and James, wounded, lonely, and deeply perplexed, felt he should consider divorce.

One day, at James's urging, he and Mai came in, presumably to discuss their problem. To begin though, James and Mai just sat on my couch, looking at me. I have got to replace that couch with armchairs, I was thinking, so couples will have to face each other instead of escaping into my face. Would that be better, or only more difficult? I will have to test this out.

Meanwhile, James and Mai were facing front. I was the point in their triangle. I fought the feeling that I was one of their kids, burdened with creating some kind of link. With my considerable prompting, we talked for almost an hour, trying to get a feel for their problems and for each other. Finally, I asked the wrong question.

"How's your sex life?"

"I don't want to talk about that," Mai said.

Silence. James had already spoken about feeling dead in the relationship, about his sense of disconnect and despair. Mai had not spoken much at all. Now this.

More silence. I tried again. "Well, could we talk about why you don't want to discuss sex?"

Mai responded instantly. "Don't give me any of that psychological crap."

Like Mai, there will be those of you who regard the self-examination necessary to identify a pattern as mere psychological crap. You are among the reactors who are far more comfortable focusing outward on concrete choices than squishing along inside, considering the slippery slopes of hidden resentments, displaced anxieties, unconscious impulses, or childhood injuries. Step four: Identify a Pattern will be tough for you, and you'll be tempted to skip it.

For a legion of others, though, the past is prologue. Many believe that by reading the past carefully, they will be offered a "get out of jail free" card. The fantasy here is something like this: I have to keep looking back, looking inside, until I find out *why*. If I understand *why* I'm anxious or afraid, then I won't be anxious or afraid anymore.

If you are that highly introspective person, then you are at risk of looking everywhere but straight ahead at the fear that needs facing. Step four: Identify a Pattern can be your sand trap because it's become a comfort zone of its own.

Somewhere between the total absorption on inner process and the utter disregard for it is the balanced assessment you'll need to ease your way out of a comfort zone. Figure out where you sit on the continuum of reflectors versus reactors and then try to move yourself closer to the middle.

Some of us are very much like Karin. We act first and wonder later how things got to be such a mess. The only thing that blasted emotionally impulsive Karin into psychotherapy was that she was unable to take a step in any new direction, and her current course was cataclysmic. Clearly it was time to call in an expert.

Jack was not bent toward reflecting on his own motives either. He always knew what he liked and set out to suit himself. While he found it troubling that so many women were upset by his agenda, he thought of it as their problem. Only Jane's obvious pain and the threat of her loss caused Jack to reexamine the life map he's been following unquestioningly.

Eventually, to make forward progress, Jack had to pause to wonder: Where did the idea of the Mercedes Man come from? What made it so attractive to him? Was it his heart's desire or an old comfort zone, romanticized but outgrown? He could only answer these questions by looking back at his life to find out how he got here.

At the other end of the reflecting pool we have Ruth, for whom looking back has been a refuge from action. Ruth would be comfortable examining her relationships with men indefinitely—lyrically faulting herself for missed opportunities and poor choices—if the conversation would delay her need to endure a blind date. Ruth will need to look back, too, not to find the flaw but to find her courage. Somewhere back there is the Ruth who took wild romantic risks, flirted with strangers, enjoyed her body. That Ruth may be buried, but she's not dead yet. Ruth needs her and she can only reconnect by looking back to where her spirited self was last sighted. Ruth could reawaken that spirit, bridle it with her hard-earned wisdom, and take herself for a hell of a ride.

What about you? If you understood why you didn't get the résumé done, though you really want to change jobs, or why you keep returning the phone calls of the friend who only makes you feel inadequate, or why you're still smoking when you absolutely definitely want to quit—if you knew why you were clinging to your own comfort trap, would that help you climb off?

Maybe. Partly. At least it's worth a try.

The Limitations of "Why"

Would Karin be able to end her triangle of romantic tension more easily if she understood what childhood pattern of love and competition made a triangle comfortable in the first place? She might, though lust is hard to resist, no matter what its psychic roots.

If James understood why the role of thwarted pursuer was so comfortable for him, would that help him make a wiser choice about the future of his marriage? Yes and no. A more complex picture of himself, his drives and unconscious choices, would certainly broaden the platform of his decision making. But James still has to bear the consequences if he chooses to dive off.

Lydia may come to realize the roots of her failure to marry, but that will only partially reduce her fears of single motherhood. In fact, if we unearth those roots too deeply or clumsily, we might make her fears worse, or weaken her nerve to go forward on her unorthodox course.

Ryan might benefit from a deeper reading of the family role he is unconsciously repeating in this second act of his life — self-defined rebel reluctant to assume the proscribed mantle of middle-class adulthood but unwilling to live without its comforts. No amount of psychic excavation, however, will automatically unlock the golden handcuffs that make him cling to his present unsatisfying circumstance.

So, know thyself, yes. But that's not all there is to it.

The power of insight to create change has passed into our cultural mythology. Since the days of *The Fifty-Minute Hour*, we've shared an entrenched belief that an insightful understanding of cause is essential to cure, or even that insight can itself provide a cure, if only that perception goes deep enough or wide enough or hits the emotional wound with enough precision. Insight has become the psychological equivalent of the elusive vaginal orgasm, so thoroughly satisfying do we imagine will be its flood of previously blocked feeling.

Even people like Mai, who resist self-disclosure or even self-discovery, usually share the general idea that there are unspoken motives behind their own and everyone else's choices. Such people may be disinclined to analyze their own motives, or refuse to reveal them on the grounds that it's nobody else's business. They may resist hearing about others' wounds, believing that most people use them as excuses for bad behavior. But even the most skeptical or biologically oriented among us don't completely doubt the power of unconscious choices, early learning, or life-long patterns. These are part of the bedrock of explanations for human behavior in our time.

Most people with whom I work, therefore, start psychotherapy with an overvalued idea of the power of *why*. The unspoken assumption is that if we look back long and hard enough to discover why a person is stuck in a comfort zone, that will go a long way toward freeing him.

It turns out that isn't true. Step four: Identify a Pattern is only one step in the seven required to get you out of your comfort zone, through that ring of anxiety, and onto higher emotional ground. The true value of recognizing your pattern is realized only when you use it in conjunction with the other six steps.

For example, when you look back at your life without first facing what hurts here and now, that backward look may mutate into blame, keeping you unproductively focused on past injury and free of personal responsibility.

If you look back without having created a motivating vision of the future, you will waste the power of that introspection to create positive change. There is only a thin distinction between self-awareness and self-absorption. Introspection *plus* your vision make you more self-aware and therefore more effective at challenging your comfort zone. Introspection without that creative vision risks sending you on a permanent double date with yourself.

Finally, if you look back without at least weighing the question of whether the time to act is now, there won't be much purpose, energy, or focus to your self-examination.

The power of *why* is therefore more limited than you may have believed. Self-scrutiny needs to occur in a context, with an emphasis on personal responsibility to avoid being sunk in blame, and with an eye toward action to avoid being stuck in the past. Supported by these twin pillars of personal responsibility and a willingness to act, however, the pattern you identify can be a critical tool for defining your path forward. *From the pattern of where you've been, you may discover where you need to go.* Plus, the very process of searching for that pattern may make it easier to move ahead.

Recognizing the *why* beneath your choices does not automatically free you to make new ones. The power of the *why* is limited by the fear that still slows you down. Despite these limitations, the payoff of *why* can be huge.

The Payoff of "Why"

Knowing more about why you are the way you are will not magically release you to act, but identifying a personal pattern does have two great rewards that make difficult action more likely:

- You can make a more conscious, more meaningful correction to your life course. Without the bigger picture of your pattern, you risk making the same mistakes again and again, and
- The process of looking back is healing in and of itself.

Anton Chekhov observed, "Man will become better when you show him what he is like." Seeing what you are like is, of course, the tricky part.

Generally speaking, we are blind to ourselves. In particular, we are blind to our individual distortions in the way we see the world. If you can recognize these warps in your own psychological lens, you can change your perceptions so they'll work better for you, help you create a new and richer comfort zone, give you a greater sense of possibility. Identifying a pattern helps you spot those distortions and so productively change your thinking and your choices.

To use a crude example, consider thirty-three-year-old Clayton; he consulted me because he was being "harassed" by colleagues at the large auction house where he had recently been promoted to the estate jewelry division. The new position required team cooperation, but Clayton was habitually standoffish, guarded with information, and suspicious of his colleagues' motives. To succeed in his new position, Clayton would have to open up to the team considerably, but it felt to him like a dumb and dangerous thing to do. His comfort zone placed him at a considerable distance from others.

Clayton presents himself, even visually, as a man who holds himself apart from the group. In the auction world of obsessively stylish people, he is some forty pounds overweight, and dresses to display it rather than disguise it. He's the sort of man who wears large pants with a belt pulled up around his armpits, giving a kind of Humpty-Dumpty effect.

His great fall would come from other people, of that Clayton had long been sure. When we took a look at Clayton's past, it was clear that he had a lifelong lens of interpersonal distrust that colored his perception of every interaction. I'm not suggesting that Clayton was crazy, far from it. But in the same way that some overly trusting people distort the world and so are easily exploited, Clayton views people through a lens tinted pale paranoid and so keeps himself at a safe distance.

When we looked back, we identified a number of factors that may have skewed his perceptions: a father who frequently warned him not to let himself get used, a manipulative older brother whose insincere charm often lulled Clayton into making a fool of himself, schoolmates who occasionally befriended brilliant Clayton only to copy his homework. Or perhaps he simply inherited his father's suspicious nature. Any or all of these early influences appear to have coalesced for Clayton in a personal truth: *People stink. Watch out.*

It cost him, of course. He was married, but they remained an emotionally isolated couple, with Clayton discouraging new friendships. He was professionally astute, knowledgeable, and dedicated, but any further professional advancement depended on his ability to tolerate and trust his colleagues. His particular distortion—that you must always be on guard, that everyone is out only for him- or herself—made collegiality impossible.

Don't miss the point. Clayton's distortion, like each of ours, is an exaggeration of some general truth, a slight warp in his wisdom. His more accurate and functional truth would be to observe that some people cannot be trusted, but some certainly can; some people will exploit you but others prefer to be fair; or, to put it in Clayton's terms, some people stink but some most assuredly do not.

For two years, Clayton and I worked weekly on making that simple shift in perception, from "watch out for all people" to "watch out for some." As Clayton began to inch toward that opening in his thinking, he was forced into new reactions. He consciously began to evaluate the genuineness of individual offers of friendship or cooperation, rather than dismissing them as generic phoniness. True, he always felt a bit triumphant when he sniffed out a scoundrel in the pack and was proven right by some later interaction. But in the process of testing his judgment, he made some risky moves toward friendship.

The steps to test his tentative new perceptions may have been modest, but the anxiety that accompanied them was predictably sharp. At first, Clayton forced himself to leave his cubicle more often, and sometimes lunched at a table with others instead of alone. He felt weird about it, but he tolerated the feeling. Then, despite mentally replaying his father's early warnings not to let himself get used, he surprised himself by offering a ride to a colleague who lived near him and had no car. Eventually this colleague, who appeared to have as keen an eye for office politics as she had for nineteenth-century jewelry, began to consider him a friend, drawing him into her office circle with traded gossip, coffee invitations, and stupid gifts exchanged on holidays.

Clayton will never be the social star of this, or probably any other, group. His basic mistrusting view of others is too entrenched to be completely abandoned. But he did eventually accomplish his goal of becoming a member of this work group, finding his own niche and taking an unexpected pleasure in his new professional comfort zone. Looking back to identify and then slightly alter his pattern was an essential step in making that change.

Clayton is an example of the rewards of identifying a pattern in conjunction with the other six steps for expanding a comfort zone:

He had faced what hurt—poor performance evaluations and the unpleasant sense that he didn't fit with his new department. (Sure, he blamed it on the group at first, calling them a "bunch of effete backstabbers" at our initial session. But looking back showed Clayton that this group was like many others he'd experienced, so perhaps what was hurting was him.)

He had created a vision of himself enjoying his colleagues and benefiting from what they had to offer, though, to be sure, initially this vision seemed absurdly far-fetched to him.

And he had reached a decision that if he was ever going to close the distance between himself and other people, the time was now. Clayton loved his job, and wanted to make the promotion work. That old, mistrustful horse he'd been hiding out on was dead. Or at least it was never going to get him where his boss told him he needed to go—inside the group and onto the team. It was time to get off.

Still, without looking back and identifying his own pattern of distortion and fear, he'd have had nowhere else to go. Once he saw, *even a little*, that perhaps his perceptions of his office mates were not entirely accurate, he could begin to face his fear by taking small risks to test those perceptions.

Like Clayton, you only have to recognize the pattern of your own distortion *a little bit*. Just glimpse a personal distortion, see a partial outline of a pattern, start to question a previously fixed assumption, and that dawning awareness may open a path in front of you. Then you can choose to let go a little, face a tolerable fear. Those small steps will move you outside your comfort zone.

More important, the classic value of looking back is its emotional release. Looking back is not merely an intellectual exercise. In the process of thinking, reflecting, and theme building, you will hit emotional pay dirt—old pain, scars of partially healed rejections, still-simmering resentments, or little-acknowledged furies. When you hit those wounds, you can repair them.

Where does our old pain go, we wonder. Into the muscles, into the nerve, pressing you to tread carefully around some issue, or forcing you to re-create a situation again and again and so give yourself another chance to make it turn out right? Touching that old pain can be healing in itself. You get to take a look at the injury with your adult eyes, to process it through all you've learned of the shades of gray in the world. When you revisit old wounds, you can knead them into a workable mass, take some of the air out, and reduce the size, scope, and power of the fear or rage that may be holding you back.

You might, like Clayton, look back at your mean and suspicious role models and call their teachings into question. Or you might regard your childhood sexual or emotional abuse through adult eyes and see finally that you were not to blame; perhaps then you can stop punishing yourself. Look back and see how the sibling who bullied you was scared herself, so maybe you can finally mend that relationship. Understand how a father's preference for your brother or a mother's depressed indifference to you might have given you a falsely diminished idea of your own worth. See the past's mark on you with fresh, grown-up eyes and it may give you a different sense of your future.

Looking back is cathartic, leaving you stronger to face your current fears. Again, understanding why you are the way you are is no trapdoor. It won't spring you free of your current comfort zone in an exhilarating rush of insight. But identifying your pattern and appreciating your own personality will certainly help point you in a direction with fresh energy and singular focus. That's what it takes to resist the pull of comfort.

Finding Your Rhyme

I don't know how clearly Mark Twain saw himself, but he certainly saw right through the rest of us. "History doesn't repeat itself," he told us, "but it rhymes."

It's the rhyme of your pattern that I'm suggesting you look for. Identifying a pattern is not a perfectly simple process, but it's not all that complicated either. I'm just recommending that you look back at your life and create a story about yourself, one that will make some kind of larger sense of the situation with which you are now struggling. You'll probably discover that you have quite a bit of that story already in place when you stop to think about it.

You do need to stop and think about it, though. And that's not easy to do. Avoidance, denial, blame, and fantasy will be at work here, too—distracting your focus, distorting your perceptions, and generally making pattern recognition far more complex than it needs to be. One of the great benefits of working with a psychotherapist to look back at your past is that the therapist acts as a counterweight to your own tendency to change the subject. A smart therapist will see the pattern even before you do, and a good one will be able to help you see it, too—see it in a palatable and productive light. These are the abilities you are paying the therapist for.

Therapy certainly can be very helpful to the process of finding the rhyme in your reasons. For some people, let's face it, it will be essential. They are simply not psychologically minded enough, not sensitive enough to emotional nuance, to spot even the beginnings of a pattern on their own. But that's not the case for most of us.

You don't need to be in therapy to ask yourself questions about your own past. It may help to set aside a specific time to focus on your answer; it would certainly be useful if you wrote those answers down because writing is a discipline that helps you to refine your thinking. And you might also want to talk your answers over with a trusted friend whose observational skills you admire. Identifying a pattern from your past is not exactly easy, but it's not impossibly arcane either. After all, we're talking about you here, and your life. Nobody is going to do *you* better.

Begin by focusing on the difficulty you are having leaving your current comfort zone. Now look back to identify your own rhyming pattern by asking yourself one or all three of these simple questions:

> Where have I done this before?
> When have I felt this before?
> Is there a familiar life theme here?

You may well have found yourself in some very similar comfort zone before, since we do tend to live our life stories over and over unless we consciously rewrite the plot. So, start with specifics.

You're thinking, "Why can't I leave my married lover?" and, if you've clung to married lovers before, look back and review the end of those affairs. What were the fears that held you in place before? Are you still behind that fence of fear today? What would you like to do differently this time?

Likewise, suppose your job is a chore and the money's not magic, so why aren't you at least calling the headhunter? First you'll review your career to see how you've pursued other opportunities. Is there a pattern you recognize? Has every job come to find you, so aggressive job-seeking behavior is outside your comfort zone? Your short story might begin, "I've never had to test myself by asking for things . . ."

Or maybe there is some more general pattern that would apply. Perhaps you notice that you are undisciplined in many aspects of your life—making lists of what you should do, then watching television instead of doing it. Your résumé is just one of many items on that list. Your story might conclude, "I have a pattern of avoiding any work I assign myself. I haven't grown into being my own boss."

It's very likely, though, that you have not challenged this specific comfort zone before. Perhaps, like James, you are considering whether to end your marriage and you have no experience of divorce. Perhaps you have never had a committee to frustrate you, so you've never faced the decision to resign. Or you are considering whether to call off the wedding, and God knows, that's a new one on you. To create his or her story, each of these people will need to look back by asking a broader question: What is there in this situation that is familiar to me?

Familiar situations tend to center around large life themes that repeatedly give you trouble, themes like separation, rejection, confrontation, competition, commitment, or fear of failure.

When you spot one of these themes in your current dilemma, look back to see how this issue has played out earlier in your life. That's where you'll find your pattern.

For example, perhaps you'll recognize that your enemy at the office provokes the same emotional response as the younger brother with whom you found it impossible to compete. They are very different adversaries, to be sure, but the whole frustrating feel of the situation helps you recognize your response pattern. You might see that you are withdrawing at the office much as you did in your family home when your brother insisted on having the bigger room or the better car. Once you identify this pattern, you might decide to reverse it. Perhaps, consciously having differentiated him from your brother, you'll befriend your would-be adversary. Or you could decide to grit your teeth and stand up to this colleague, insisting on getting your share of the project or the credit. Identifying your old family pattern in this new setting, familiar in feeling if not in specific fact, may inspire you to make better choices this time around.

Or maybe you are a divorced mom, uncomfortable disciplining your teenage daughter for fear she will make good on her threat to go live with her father. Ask yourself how you've dealt with your fear of rejection before. Has it kept you from doing what's right or what's best? Could you challenge that fear more successfully this time?

Suppose you do ninety percent of the family work and your husband does ten. You resent it bitterly, but you feel unable to confront him effectively. Look back and I'll bet you'll note that you usually are more comfortable being the angry martyr than being the target of someone's anger. Identifying that pattern will help you to recognize that you will never get your fair share in life if you don't insist on it, even though insistence is apt to make your partner mad. (You are asking him to tolerate change and that makes most of us angry, no matter how justified that change might be.) Leave your safe, resentful comfort zone and tolerate his displeasure, because you've lived out this pattern long enough.

If you feel stuck in some system where you feel oppressed—your corporation, for example, or the school system, or your custody proceedings—look back to see where else you have struggled against feeling powerless in your life. Has it overwhelmed you? A look back can mobilize your creative problem solving when looking around only makes you feel trapped.

Find the rhyme in your pattern by generalizing from your specific situation to some larger theme or familiar feeling and use these as a bridge to your past. Then tell a little story about yourself that explains your current comfort zone in terms of your lifelong pattern of behavior. It will help to frame your story with sentences like:

"I always . . ." ("I always end up as a caretaker because I feel like I won't be left" might be the short story of a woman struggling with whether to leave her alcoholic partner.)

"I never . . ." ("I never take orders from myself, because all my energy goes into rebelling against someone else's orders" might be part of the pattern Ryan observes when he tries to focus on his self-defeating procrastination.)

"I need to . . ." ("I need to stop looking for someone to take care of me" might help a woman who keeps connecting with controlling partners finally establish an equal relationship.)

It should be clear from this discussion that looking back is a very inexact science. The first problem is that there is *no single right answer to any of the questions you ask.* A life pattern is comprised of an almost infinite number of elements and the rhyme that emerges depends entirely on where you choose to focus as you question yourself. No pattern that you define is *the one*, and it's always useful to remember that there are others waiting to be explored at another moment or when you are facing a different dilemma.

Also, you are too complex, your motives too intertwined to pull out one thread and say "Aha"—here is *the* cause of my fear, the root of my insecurity, the fuel for my jealousy. Even if you can recognize one traumatic incident or a single troubled situation that has cast a long shadow over your life, your understanding of those pivotal events may change as you work through them.

Shawna, for example, was assaulted and raped when she was a senior in high school. For the next decade she avoided men, attributing both her fear and self-loathing to the trauma of that event. As we worked together, she began to understand that her anxiety around men and her discomfort with herself long predated the rape. That horrifying experience froze her feelings in place, but it did not completely cause them. Nor was she doomed by the rape to see herself as a victim forever. Rape was an evil thing that happened from which she came to believe she could recover. Developing a different version of the effects of her traumatic experience gave Shawna a different and deeper understanding of herself. And from the fresh understanding eventually came the possibility of new choices and happier possibilities.

So there's more than one right answer to the general question: Where have I done this before/felt this before/wrestled with these issues before? There are, however, better answers. You'll recognize those better answers as ones that will help you:

- See your current dilemma through a wider-angle lens.

- Focus your energy on an internal, developmental goal.
- Decide what to do next and have the courage to do it.

Here's a simple example: "I know I should fire these employees but I can't seem to get myself to do it" feels stuck. Look back to put your dilemma in a larger and more useful context. Ask "Have I ever done this before?" and you answer a tentative "yes." Perhaps, though you've never had to fire anyone, you realize that you have always dreaded giving an employee negative feedback.

Do you recognize the feelings? A more definite yes. Maybe you'll observe, "The idea makes me anxious. I was the baby and the family pet. I just hate it when people don't like me."

Is there a familiar theme in this dilemma? Yes again. "I avoid confrontations. I can think of past situations where that avoidance has cost me plenty, and I don't want to make those mistakes again. These two employees present an opportunity to get past my fear." Now you have a decision to act and an internal goal (finding the courage to face confrontation) to further motivate that action.

Looking back to identify your pattern of avoiding confrontation and analyzing the roots of that avoidance is no guarantee that you will actually take steps to fire the slackers. But it will certainly increase your odds. Combine that looking back with a structured plan to face what hurts, a vision of the kind of person you are hoping to become (one who is a better and stronger manager), and you are out of your comfort zone and closer to where you want to be.

But those were not the only answers you might have given. You might have considered your reluctance to fire those employees through a different lens and made other, equally valid observations of your own life patterns. Possibly you'd detect a history of insecurity that makes you more comfortable with less competent employees who don't threaten you. You might also recognize that you are most comfortable in the role of caretaker, only at ease giving more than you get. Any of these patterns might focus your attention on useful internal goals and motivate you to fire those employees, fueled, though, by a different cauldron of courage.

Many rhymes, and therefore right answers, can satisfy those same three goals—see your comfort zone in a wider context, identify some internal developmental goal, and decide on your next, risky action.

Note, too, that *a pattern is not necessarily a problem*. Every comfort zone does not automatically need to be challenged, and life patterns are certainly not always evidence of dysfunction. You might, for example, observe your pattern as a caretaker, decide that you don't aspire to be a person who is comfortable firing two employees, and instead work harder to help those goof-offs improve their job performance. Some comfort zones continue to be a good fit.

You can identify your pattern and choose to change it, learn your pattern and come to recognize its value to you, or something in between. The point is that there is a pattern to your choices, a coherence to your life story, a comfortable way of seeing and being that feels like you. That pattern is an important part of the psychological comfort zone we discussed in Chapter One. Remember, you'll probably always do what you always did, unless you make a focused and conscious leap to do something different.

Look Back, but Don't Stare

There are risks, of course, in looking back. Looking back does generally include your childhood, especially your parents — their relationship to you, to your siblings, and to each other — because your family is, in fact, the first footprint in the wet cement of your psyche. And an examination of childhood is often an invitation to blame.

As Hobbes advised Calvin in his cartoon advice about writing a self-help book, people mostly want to know that they are not to blame. The most gratifying way of escaping one's own sense of responsibility is to find someone else to hold that hot potato. An objective and thoughtful look back at your childhood will necessarily demonstrate that other people's actions had enormous impact on you and, because they were only human, some of that impact was probably negative. It can be a short hop from that recognition to blame.

Sometimes it's less painful to recognize your own distortions when you can hold someone else to blame for them. When Clayton could identify his father's fears and his brother's manipulations, it was easier for him to identify his own misguided views. To the degree that blaming your parents or other caretakers allows you to drop your defenses and look hard in the mirror, temporary blame can be a useful tool. If you linger in blame much more than temporarily, though, you are staring backward. Unstuck is always straight ahead.

It is certainly possible to identify a pattern, looking back into childhood for its roots, without getting stuck in a whirlpool of blame. Here's how we used Karin's early life to help clarify her decisions about Marshall and Dr. Bob:

Beginning with the question "Where have I done this before?" it seemed reasonable to look back at the underlying pattern of Karin's relationships with men. She began by asking "Where have I been in a triangle before?" and then "When have I felt these feelings before?" The answers came pretty quickly.

The whole tale of Karin and men is a *War and Peace*–length saga, similarly themed and stocked with characters only a Russian novelist or an obsessive manager like Karin could paint in detail. But the bottom line about Karin and men is as simple and unsurprising as *Goodnight Moon*. Start talking to Karin about her pattern with men and you are instantly talking about Dad. Dad and the brothers. The king and his princes. And one very special, very gifted, very pretty, and very competitive princess—Karin.

Karin is the third of four children, with three brothers, one magnificently removed, hugely successful workaholic father, and a mother who ruled in his absence but caved completely when Dad came through the door. So, in fact, did Karin, who was otherwise a fairly assertive, tomboyish friend and pet to her brothers. This was a house in which even Mom wanted to be Dad, where being male was king and pleasing males makes you queen. Karin grew up trying to be both king and queen and she did a marvelous job at both.

As an adult she has continued to shine in both roles, albeit in a rigidly compartmentalized way. She continues her successful competition with prince surrogates at work and pleases them in bed at night. It's a system Karin has down pat but it no longer works for her. It's interfering with her ability to marry and become a mother. She has outgrown this familiar comfort zone, but she's stuck.

In our conversations, we looked back at Karin's past with an emphasis on understanding what it says about her current dilemma. For example, I ask her to wonder why Marshall, of all the men, is the one to whom she got engaged. Turns out that he isn't the first fiancé she's had. In her early twenties there was a similarly sweet and successful Alan, who gave her a ring before he eventually gave up on getting her to the altar. But the pattern of finding Mr. Nice and distracting herself with Mr. Powerful was well established.

We develop the dynamic explanation that Marshall, Alan, and a number of other acceptable boyfriends in whom Karin lost interest but to whom she stayed connected until she could get them to dump her are all sibling relationships for Karin. They are her equals, her brothers, partners, and playmates whom she respects and admires, loves and appreciates. When they love and support her, too, the relationships are very important. But they are not now and probably never will be any contest for Dad, the king.

Bob is king, compared with Marshall's perfectly acceptable prince. When Bob made his sexual offer, he was too powerful to refuse. Yet Marshall is too companionable to lose. Besides, in a heartfelt and completely realistic sense, Karin is exhausted competing with the boys. She wants the maternal glory of being a girl. Marshall is the only one who will give her the child she craves. An offer she couldn't refuse. A fiancé she doesn't want to lose. Stuck.

As a daughter, Karin could dump her brothers for Dad at any opportunity. In fact, she and I spend some time looking back, confirming that was exactly what she did. As a girlfriend, she plays out the same drama in a painfully confusing fashion. Karin may have the same conflicting needs for the king and the prince, but she'll have to find new ways to satisfy them.

Karin began to accept her need for a powerful male figure to love and admire. She saw that she identified with her mother as much as she competed with her, and that she could have her own king without betraying her love for her dad. Then she could become a mother and have the family she longed for. Karin came to see that there was nothing wrong with these aspirations, whether or not her parents or any surrogate parent blessed them.

Identifying her pattern helped Karin to accept that, much as she wants to be a wife and mother, she can't be satisfied with a sibling figure like Marshall as her life partner. He's a lovely man, she is loath to hurt him more, but she recognized that she will always be seeking a powerful male figure, like Dr. Bob, to be her life partner. Of course she's known all along that Dr. Bob had to go. He's married, and besides, unlike Dad, Bob is not very nice.

Karin's look back made it clear that her next step forward required letting both men go.

CHAPTER 7

LET GO

Amy's daughter invited her stepmother to help choose her wedding dress because "After all, Dad's the one paying for the wedding." This newest slight was heaped on five years of similar insults and omissions. Still, Amy was staggered by this further evidence of the loss of her daughter's love since the divorce. Amy, who left the comfort zone of a financially secure, emotionally barren marriage, is paying an unexpectedly high price for it. As her own mother meanly reminds her, "Be careful what you wish for."

For five years Amy has been ensnared in a hopeless competition with her ex-husband over their children. Where Amy makes financial suggestions to her children, her ex simply clears up their credit card debt. When she offers Thanksgiving dinner, her ex counters with a Thanksgiving cruise. She is losing this brutal tug-of-war. Amy has come to psychotherapy to figure a way to win her children back. I already know she has to let them go. But how?

Everything you give up hurts. This is your next hurdle.

You have faced your dissatisfaction and envisioned a change. You have decided the time is now. You have identified some relevant pattern in your past and you are using it to map your next move.

Now you will probably begin to grapple with the terrible specifics. When do I quit the job? How do I tell my husband I'm gay? Do I move out first or see the lawyer? Cut off the relationship cleanly or ease out slowly? Just close the business and walk away or take in a partner and change our focus? See my husband through rehab, see the kids through high school, hold off until I'm vested, quit first, look first, confront first, what's first?

You appear to be asking yourself, How should I make the move, and when? But there is a common, unspoken meaning behind your question, one that needs to be addressed: How should I do it so it doesn't hurt?

The hard answer will bring you to a temporary standstill. You can't.

You knew that, of course, though most of us freeze in place when we first confront this truth. Letting go is a normal, even inevitable process, yet it nearly always bruises. We've learned this because all of growing up occurs through a series of losses, and each one leaves a scar. Those ground rules of adulthood are no less difficult for any one of us merely by virtue of being universal. They consist of simple, unpleasant truths:

- Childhood ends without our having received everything we needed.

- We are responsible for ourselves and a great deal more, whether we choose to be or not.
- We are flawed, limited, and time is very short.
- We will never be perfectly loved; in fact, as it's said, nobody every loved anybody the way everybody wants to be loved.
- We will lose those we love in many different ways and forever mourn their loss.
- We will be forced to let go of people and things we cherish in order to move forward on our path. Worse still, we will be forced as adults to *decide* who and what to let go of, and so inflict our own suffering and theirs.

This last is the point at which ex-wife Amy is faltering. She recognizes the costs of her broken family's loyalty war. She has kept count of every injury: the twenty-first birthday to which she was not invited because "Dad and Marilyn would have been uncomfortable," the graduation where she sat alone ("Don't guilt-trip us! Didn't we spend the night before with you?"), the bitter confrontations over holidays when her kids failed to choose her, or worse, her guilty awareness that they would suffer for the times they did. The competition is ugly, unloving, and in her power to stop, but only if she lets go.

Amy loves her children, loathes their father. Letting go of the battle that is wounding her kids means allowing their father to win. Necessary as it seems to give up her struggle, it also seems impossible.

Karin, too, is struggling against the wrenching need to inflict her own loss. She believes she must give up both Marshall and

Bob, because she will never create a satisfying life with one or a safe life with the other. But it is a huge leap from seeing to separating. How can she relinquish the possibility of a child with Marshall? How can she deliberately say no to the satisfactions of sexual passion with Bob?

And what is the next layer down that Karin would have to leave behind? Dramatic chaos? The familiar feeding frenzy that being the only girl in a world of attentive, competitive men promotes? The hunger for a powerful daddy? Whatever the wellspring of her profound attachment to each of these men, how can she willfully transcend it?

We can understand the strength of Karin's romantic ties even if neither can offer her long-term happiness. We can accept Amy's reluctance to abandon her battle for her children's affections even though the struggle itself is hopeless and demeaning to boot. But what about those people who appear to cling to utterly unrewarding situations, exploitive friendships, or destructive relationships? Why can't they let go?

Why did your friend complain for a year about her controlling boyfriend and then become engaged to him? Why does a man like Ryan, frustrated with the family business since high school, still make it his life's work? Why do you keep having lunch with the friend who only picks your brain and then leaves you to pick up the check?

The fact is, it's tough to let go *even when it's not clear what the rewards are for staying put*. Attachments put down roots and digging those roots up is unpleasant, even when you are transplanting yourself to Eden.

What Breaks Your Heart

The most trivial of disturbed roots tweaks us. Change your bank, switch dentists, try a new supermarket or a different commute to work and many of us will have a small but noticeable emotional response. People report a tiny pinch ("I've been banking there forever") or a disloyal jolt ("He wasn't a very good dentist, but I hated to hurt his feelings") when letting go.

We feel the twinge even at moments of welcome change. It is your unanticipated pang when, in the weeks before the move to a new home, old neighbors suddenly feel like cherished friends. It is the small sadness at your office going-away party, making you momentarily wish you weren't leaving at all. It is the lump in your throat at the airport, though you'd counted the days until your parents went back home. Attachments may be thin or conflicted, but they still throb when they are endangered.

These are the stabs of small losses, noticeable yes, but still easily overcome with exchanges of phone numbers, addresses, lunch dates, and other tokens of reunion that ease the transition. Still, consider how even these invisible roots make their presence felt when they are displaced and you can appreciate what it feels like to deliberately let go of a marriage, a job, a child, a habit, a company, or a friend.

It might feel impossible to you, too.

Confronting that fearsome pain, we blink backward, clutching harder where we intended to let go, worrying that the loss will be regrettable, even unendurable. Forty-one-year-old Nita, contemplating divorce, was struck by the surprising force of her paralysis. "I was always the one to tell people, 'If you're not happy, leave him! Life's too short.' My God, I even said that to people with kids, can you imagine? Now I try walking in those shoes and I can't take a step. I wake up and look around and what I feel is panic. I'd be leaving everything we built in eleven years—our house, the family room we haven't even paid for yet—and not just the house but all our friends and the memories. I'll have to destroy all of that. Is being unhappy enough of a reason?"

Nita is envisioning her loss. Imagined loss is sometimes worse than the actual experience, like those smokers whose vision of a morning coffee without a cigarette is so bleak, they cannot conceive of a reason to wake up. Yet some do quit and discover that the morning and the coffee are still there and still sweet, even in the absence of their beloved nicotine. Likewise unhappy lovers, who nonetheless cling to a relationship because they are afraid of being alone, may discover that alone is a relief after the chaos of attached. It is that potential for pain, rather than the pain itself, that makes most of us so fearful.

Envisioning loss is looking into the abyss. How do we bring ourselves to jump? Maybe the prospect of pain means we should stay where we are? Or maybe it means we will stay where we are whether we should or not, simply because we cannot imagine enduring it.

Every person who is pressing him- or herself toward change eventually hits the hard wall of this emotional reality: Change requires letting go of the status quo, with all the sweet rewards sprinkled through its stifling limits. That loss hurts. Even a dead horse looks like a beloved pet when you contemplate saying good-bye.

One element makes letting go particularly torturous, more so, say, than facing what hurts initially or confronting fear down the line. For some it is this last element that finally breaks our heart, namely, the pain that our letting go will inflict on the person or group we will leave.

Call your overwhelming feeling neurotic guilt or moral obligation. Call it integrity or martyrdom or call it love. Whatever you call it, however you judge it, it's there, it exists, and it puts a price on letting go that some deem too high to pay.

Unhappily married James hit a tsunami of guilt when he floated the idea of leaving his wife after four months of psychotherapy. "I can't even allow the thought of leaving her to be in my mind. How would she eat? Who would get food for the kids? How could she handle her job, plus everything I do at home? I imagine leaving but coming back every weekend to cook and do the laundry, to make sure she's OK. How could I hurt her that much? Am I justified in destroying all that? Why can't I find a way to be happy here?"

James's fantasy—that he could let go but still take care—is a common wish that surfaces when we confront the pain we will inflict. Some of us act out that wish, half-leaving, half-staying, a leg in each separating canoe, pinioned by guilt and unable to get a solid balance.

Audrey broke up with her girlfriend Liz last year, but still spends every weekend sleeping on Liz's fold-out couch. Why? "I'm too guilty to turn down the invitation. I can't stand to hurt her."

Gary told Celeste it was over six months ago. But he still takes her almost daily phone calls, when she alternately asks a favor, pleads for an explanation, or vents her fury. His willingness to stay connected to Celeste makes his new girlfriend wary and strains the possibilities of their relationship, but Gary feels helpless to hang up on Celeste. "We were together three years," he explains, "and she says I've ruined her life. I just can't be so cold as to slam down the phone. I'm hoping she'll just get tired of calling." So far, she hasn't.

Professional attachments can be as compelling and as guilt-provoking as romantic relationships. Kenya, twenty-eight, is the den mother, producer, and heartbeat of a small thriving theatrical improv company that she founded after college. She's been offered a solid sitcom part in Los Angeles, which would be a huge boost for her and probably a deathblow to her theater company. What does she owe the actors she has drawn to her? What does she owe herself?

When one member of an advertising team is offered a better job, does he turn away from his partner and take it? When athletic partners could do better elsewhere, do they serve themselves or each other? Do the strong, with more opportunities, owe nothing to their needier partners? Do they owe everything? Where do you draw your line?

The heartbreaking aspect of letting go is not just what you yourself will suffer. After all, you stand to gain, too. The killer is that someone you value, someone you owe, or someone you love will lose alongside you, and he or she will not share in the compensating gains. When you are in the tight grasp of guilt and obligation, you understand the worst of letting go. Your only choice is either to stay where you are and make peace with your obligation and commitment, or free yourself of its grip and do your best to ease the injuries your freedom has inflicted on others.

Your choice will depend in part on your situation and on the actions and attitudes of the other people involved. But much of your choice will depend on you, and the way you form attachments. The fact is, everybody's roots don't go equally deep.

"Is It Cold in Here, or Is It You?"

How did Anna get on that boat and sail off to tutor the children of the king of Siam? Why wasn't she held in place by the belief that if she left England, she'd never find a new husband who lived in the right neighborhood? I have plenty of patients who can't leave Cherry Hill, New Jersey, for that reason.

What allowed Jimmy Carter's mother, Miz Lillian, to leave her perfectly cozy peanut farm and join the Peace Corps, at an age when many of her peers find unseasonable weather too challenging? An inborn spirit of adventure, or lifelong lessons in letting go and moving on?

What emboldened Pamela Churchill to charm her father-in-law Winston sufficiently to ensure her introduction to Averill and the rest? Was she born with the ability to use and lose her conjugal baggage, or did she learn how to let go when the going was good?

Practicing in Philadelphia, where it is common for three generations to shop at the same deli, I find that enduring attachments and the agony of loss are largely the way of the emotional world. That depth of attachment and pain of separation, however, are highly subject to individual difference.

I think first of my friend Terry, who mentioned as we were shoe shopping that she had been having sexual fantasies about men other than her husband. Two weeks later she left her husband. Just like that. No therapy, no obvious angst, no ambivalent sexual reunion with him a month later, just left him and filed for divorce. Her ability to let go was breathtaking to me.

Three years later Terry repeated herself, moving out of a

lover's apartment when she decided that he had a drinking problem and she didn't want her life to be about alcoholism. Period.
She didn't go the usual save-the-sinner, how could I leave him
when he's ill, besides I can't leave him, I love him route. She
made a decision and she left. Wow.

Terry later married someone else. I don't know if she is still
married, because some time after the wedding, she dumped me,
too. I always think of her, though, as an example of the ease with
which some people can let go.

Where do you consider yourself to be on this continuum between some people's steadfast reach for the comfort of familiar
body heat and Terry's cool, evaluative detachment? We are all
somewhere on that scale. At the extremes, there are men and
women so crippled by separation pain that they cannot let a
beloved out of the room or into a friendship without feeling the
threat of loss. And there are certainly people more disconnected
than Terry, people for whom any emotional bond is anathema,
people who have sexual partners instead of relationships, or who
seek no one at all. Considering this broad spectrum of attachment patterns, where would you place yourself?

For example, if you are stuck today in the job you've been
thinking of leaving for years, take a look around you. Have others
jumped ship? I'll bet they have. Where did they land? Are they
happier now, freer, more satisfied, more financially secure? I'll
bet many of them are. How come you're the one still sitting on
the safe wasp's nest of discontent, shifting around uncomfortably,
but still sitting, sitting? Probably, at least in part, because you
haven't learned how to force yourself to separate. If the office
doesn't push you out, and you don't learn to let go on your own,
you'll be clinging to this lifeline indefinitely.

What about the house that you've complained is too small,

though the effort to relocate is too great? Or the wedding plans marching inexorably along, though the marriage looms ever more ominously as it approaches? Can you quit the tennis team that is no longer fun, though your father, who expects to root proudly for years to come, will be hurt and disappointed? Will you trail forever in your older brother's protective footsteps, though his decisions don't take you where you really want to go? Each of these is an instance where the strength to let go may be the deciding factor.

There's a learning curve to letting go and we all start with greater or lesser aptitude for the subject. Amy is an example of someone who started out at one end of the spectrum. Here's how she learned what she needed.

What You Wish For

Amy left a financially secure marriage, demonstrating now and forever that she has more than her share of the ability to let go. As you'll see, though, some of the issues that kept her too long in her marriage have resurfaced, making it very tough to let go of her current battleground. This time she feels she'd be giving up on her children, and that's much tougher for her than was leaving the husband she had come to despise.

By the time we met, Amy had faced the ugliness of her family battles. She knows what hurts. But the vision of letting go, only to settle for scraps from her children's table, is intolerable to her. Right now, that's the only outcome she can foresee if she stops pursuing her kids and waits for them to come to her. Amy needs to create a positive vision in order to steel herself to let go.

Looking back actually helped to break Amy's deadlock. A

child of divorce who was desperate to create her own happy family, Amy realized that she had tried to build a family using the same raw materials that had failed for her own mother, namely a glamorous, angry, and distant husband. Amy chose a husband much like her own dad, and spent her marriage trying to get this father substitute to love her the way her own dad surely did not.

Neither did her husband, who lost interest in her shortly after he won her and moved on to other women and other challenges. He was outraged, though, when Amy finally divorced him, furious that she had disrupted his comfortable life and dealt him a public rejection. Their divorce battle was brutal, in part because her ex appeared to set out deliberately to win the hearts of his kids.

The father who could never remember the names of their teachers was transformed into the super-dad who lovingly wanted to solve his children's every little problem—with a gift, a treat, a special vacation with their friends. Amy could not compete but she could complain. She did, and it only made things worse.

Her daughter was especially appreciative of all this daddy devotion and she treated Amy with the same dismissive contempt that her dad had modeled for years. Amy found herself in her old pattern, this time with her child. She was running after her distant daughter, doing little errands ("Mom, could you pick me up a pair of black stockings—I can't leave work"), currying favor. Instead of appreciation, she got heaved aside ("No, you can't stay at my place while your apartment's being painted. Don't you have any friends?"). If Amy complained, that made her a whiner. If she refused to do the favors, that made her a bitch. Amy was stuck in a familiar pattern of pursuit and abuse.

Identifying her pattern helped strengthen Amy's conviction that, whatever else, she needed to stop repeating the same old dead-end behavior with her daughter that she had developed first with her own father and then relived with her husband. Pursuing love from a critic just won't work. What might?

Amy needed to open up some room for a vision to develop. If only she could let go just a little. What helped Amy, and what might help you, too, was to gain a deeper appreciation of letting go. What might initially feel only like loss can actually come to seem a more mature version of love.

To see loss through these developmental eyes, you need to appreciate three less obvious facets of letting go:

- Letting go is not necessarily giving up.
- Letting go is not necessarily all or nothing.
- Letting go might mean individuation rather than separation.

If any of these apply to your situation, it could ease your exit considerably.

Letting Go Is Not Losing All

Letting go initially seemed impossible to Amy because she confused it with giving up her desire to be close to her children. "I could never stop wishing for that," she said, so how could she stop fighting for it, no matter how destructive the war? But letting go is not the same as giving up. Rather, letting go may mean *recognizing the difference between what you can and cannot control.*

Amy's intense emotional focus on her children maximizes her pain, but it doesn't make the kids turn to her any more frequently. The sad fact is that nothing Amy does can make the kids want to be close to her. For Amy, letting go means facing that painful reality and ceasing to pursue a goal that, when she chases it, only seems to slip farther away.

It's a nuance, but a crucial one. Letting go does not mean giving up desire, necessarily, nor does it have to mean giving up on ever having that desire fulfilled. It means letting go of the behaviors you've been using to get to that goal because you recognize they aren't working for you.

Marriage, for example, is a goal some relinquish without giving up on the idea of marriage someday. One woman told me she used her thirty-fifth birthday to do just that: "This year for my birthday I decided to stop worrying about whether or not I'm going to get married. I'm going to stop Internet dating or going to singles events. I took stock and saw that they make me feel bad. I'd like to be married, that's for sure. But I can't make it happen, or if I maybe could, I'd have to do all these things I simply no longer want to do. I've been wondering what I might put in place of the marriage goal, and right now I don't know. But that's OK. I figure as long as I stick with my resolution to stop worrying about it, I'll see other things happen in my life."

I think she will, too. Let go of one frantic pursuit, and it leaves room for fresh desire.

It was easy for Amy to recognize that she couldn't control her children's affections, but difficult for her to stop trying. She was comforted by the idea that she didn't have to give up hope of someday connecting with the kids more intimately, though she did have to let go of her furious contest with their dad. By distinguishing between letting go and giving up entirely, she was able to take a longer view of their relationships. She doesn't have to let go of her children per se. She just has to let go of the battle in which her relationship with them is the greatest casualty.

Letting Go Is Not All or Nothing

In many situations, letting go is more of a gradual process than a wrenching moment of pain. You might tell the boyfriend who won't come up with the ring that time is running out, perhaps break up and then reconcile two or three times, before you can finally bring yourself to issue the ultimatum with which you can stick.

You could gradually test a few independent decisions, but still run the crucial ones by the parent who dominates your life. Over time, you test more and more of your ability to leave that protected comfort zone and create a new one under your own umbrella.

Many leave the marriage long before divorcing the mate, uncoupling in a slow establishment of separate interests, separate relationships, then separate finances, and finally separation. Likewise, you might abandon the comfort zone of your single life and merge as a comfortable couple only in gradual stages, letting go of one slowly as you cross the bridge into a new arena. Job change and retirement allow for letting go in pieces, too. People plan partial retirements or prepare for career change in night school while maintaining a secure day job.

Some even test new identities without abandoning the old ones. For example, Diane, the dancer, became a college student by day and remained an exotic dancer by night. Exotic dancing was far more than Diane's source of income. It was her world, her comfort zone. The life of college student was an uncomfortable leap for her—the people, the routine, the studying, actually her whole sense of self felt like a clumsy fit. Financially she could afford to be a full-time student, but psychologically it was too great a leap. So we inched her into her new comfort zone, beginning with just one course a semester, which would not interfere with her work schedule.

By summer session Diane had doubled her academic load and reduced her dance hours. The following fall she was a full-time student, though she danced on holiday breaks—in her mind to get some extra cash, in mine because she didn't want to lose touch with her old self completely. Eventually, as Diane relinquished her former comfortable role and invested in her new identity, she elaborated a vision of her future that was a blend of the two. Diane has set her sights on business school, with the goal of owning her own strip club someday. ("Gentleman's Club," she is always reminding me.) Like I said, letting go is not necessarily all or nothing.

It must be noted that when you only let go partway, you do risk becoming stuck in your old comfort zone indefinitely. Some relationships, whether professional or personal, are best ended by amputation—one clean chop and then wait for the throbbing to subside. Halfway measures may become dead ends, as when cherished romances sputter into "friendships" whose true translation is an exiting partner too guilty to turn away completely and a rejected partner holding on to hope under another name.

For the exiting partner, the proffer of "friendship" can be a good way to let go slowly of one comfort zone while building a new nest elsewhere. For the clinging partner, though, the "friendship" is like a bankrupt business that opens the next day under another name. It's legal, but is it right?

Long after divorce, some of us stay married by continuing to rely on that ex-spouse for life support, speaking daily or calling regularly in a crisis. Amy and I even wondered whether her battle with her ex was a way to stay connected to him. (The very thought, stated openly, motivated her to move on.)

On a limited basis, an ongoing connection with a former lover or mate is a lovely outcome, a neat salvage job of the best of a sinking relationship. It can be costly, though, because it risks allowing you to cling to an old comfort zone at the expense of new relationships. If you're caught here and you take a careful look, you can probably tell the difference.

Amy was encouraged by the notion of letting go as a gradual process. For her it meant that every new issue—a son's phone call she expected that didn't come, an upcoming birthday, a new request for a favor—was an opportunity to practice letting go of her competition with her ex. If she reacted in her old anxious, guilt-provoking way, well, there would be a new opportunity to try again next week. Gradually she'd get better at assuming her new stance.

Letting Go May Mean Individuation Rather Than Separation

What finally moved Amy forward, though, was when she came to see that letting go does not have to mean loss of the relationship. Alternatively, it might mean *individuation*—that is, letting go by allowing someone close to you to become his or her own distinct person, however different from you.

In theory, individuation is a perfectly obvious—and obviously necessary—part of any developing attachment. Love a child but let that child become his own person, right? Adore a mate but allow that mate to be himself or herself. Cherish a sibling but respect that sibling's right to differ on fundamental life issues. Who could disagree, in theory at least?

In real experience, though, a beloved's individuation may be hurtful or infuriating. Let a child individuate by marrying outside her race or religion, and some parents will have a little trouble comfortably letting go. Let a mate express himself with fart jokes at your office Christmas party and it may not be easy to remember that he is, after all, a separate individual from you and entitled to his own social judgment. Have a sibling become rabidly religious or politically extreme and it may be difficult to accept this new attitude with equanimity.

Cherished people test our attachments by developing in ways that are different from what we expect or need them to be. In other words, wrong ways. We try to pull them back into the old comfort zone we once shared—pointing out to the daughter that she mustn't marry outside the family comfort zone's perimeter, reviewing and rebuking the husband in a vain effort to make his behavior conform with our comfort, trying to talk the sibling back into who he or she used to be.

Individuation means that these close people have abandoned the comfort zone we shared with them, leaving a hole where we once enjoyed a heartbeat. Letting go here does not have to mean losing the person. But it does mean losing the comfortable connection we once enjoyed and accepting this new, different person he or she has become. In these instances, letting go is not so much a loss as a long, long stretch.

Amy had a focusing moment that helped her to appreciate, in a gut emotional way, her children's needs as distinct from her own. She had a share in a singles' beach house, and sitting with new friends, she watched a boat sail past that she recognized as her ex-husband's. Her children were probably on that boat, she thought, and waited to feel left out. But she didn't.

Instead, she recognized that she was satisfied with where she was, and that her children were in a very different emotional place. "They are in pursuit of their father's money, his charisma, his approval, his love—just like I used to be. Look how long it took me to give that up. Maybe they will never stop chasing him. Maybe they will be more successful in getting love from him than I ever was. I can't be angry with them for hungering after something I also wanted so much, for so long. I have to let go of my hurt feelings and go get another life. My kids will love me when they can."

That revelation helped Amy create a vision of herself as a compassionate harbor for her children, a place they could go for solace when the grail of their father's interest and approval proved an exhausting quest. She would take a small step toward this vision by no longer allowing herself to be used by her daughter as a servant, realizing that no one turns for comfort to one they demean. She would abandon her martyred complaints ("Marilyn better not be in more wedding pictures than I am") and replace them with direct statements of her feelings ("I want to let you know that participating in the wedding pictures is important to me").

Amy's goal was to stop wooing and pursuing her kids—not to reject them in anger, but simply to pull back, let go, and wait for them to return in their own way and time. She is letting go, but letting go without giving up hope, letting go in tolerable stages, letting go of expectations and anger without letting go of the children themselves.

You, too, have a vision in mind, a goal toward which you are heading when you leave this comfort zone. Actively work toward letting go of the ties holding you back by asking yourself three questions:

- From whom or what must I separate and what must I lose?

- Who am I trying to protect, and how will my progress hurt him or her?
- Finally, and most important, what will make the loss more tolerable?

Three Questions

What Will I Have to Give Up?

See yourself right now, standing at the edge of your platform, looking ahead to the vision you have created. Notice that you are not standing freely on that platform. You are tied there.

Your most immediate ties are perfectly apparent, because you feel them consciously and acutely. These emotional attachments form tendrils around your courage, squeezing it limp. You don't have to wonder what they are; you feel their anchoring power.

So, to the question "What do I have to let go of?" Amy's first mournful answer is "My kids." Karin flatly lists both Bob and Marshall. Ryan points right to his checkbook, a grim recognition of his attachment to a soft life that he fears would be lost, despite his dissatisfactions with it. You might have an immediate answer, too, identifying the marriage you will poison if you choose the new lover, or the secure salary you must abandon if you want the sexy job.

Next, you might examine your answer more closely in an effort to understand the true scope of your loss, neither inflating it nor minimizing it. That won't be true for everyone. Karin insisted that itemizing her losses would not make it easier to pull away from either Bob or Marshall. On the other hand, close scrutiny helped Amy to realize that she did not have to let go of her kids so much as she had to let go of her expectations of them, which would certainly be tough enough. In the end, though, her loss would be smaller than she had feared.

I asked Ryan to put his financial loss into concrete numbers because, after all, if money has you tied to a comfort zone, it's wise to know the price of freedom. Ryan figured in both salary and his share of the inheritance that would be lost if he left the family business now. His final figure was impressive enough to make both of us take a second look at his situation. While it was possible, it was unlikely that Ryan could achieve that level of financial security in an independent career. Was he stuck?

No. He was finally, as he put it, "getting real."

Mapping out Ryan's potential financial losses helped him let go of his half-stoned, "someday I'll just walk out of here" fantasy. Given his financial interest, Ryan immediately decided that, realistically, he was not walking out of anywhere. Money was too high on his list of what matters. Now his choices are more clear. He can stay stuck in his unsatisfying role of family screwup and keep collecting his paycheck, or he can let go of that role and take more risk and more responsibility, create a new role and a more satisfying comfort zone right in the company.

Ryan's satisfaction requires letting go of a more subtle sort. Some powerful attachments, like those to familiar roles or beliefs, lurk beneath the conscious surface and are especially difficult to renounce because they are invisible and elusive. Underground and amorphous, worn roles and fixed ideas can nonetheless be superglue.

Prime among these limiting beliefs might be your investment in your own self-image. Ryan sees himself as too cool for his box business and too creative for its tedious paperwork. He resists his work because it's an ego pinch, and that makes it impossible for him to take pleasure in it or turn his true creative talents toward it.

You, too, may have an idea of yourself that limits your possibilities for change. The fact is, you can cherish an image of yourself as passionately as you might another person. And either might be a bad relationship.

> I can't quit my job, no matter how difficult my life, because I just don't see myself as a stay-at-home mother.
> I need a steady income, but I'm much too artistic to hold a corporate job.
> My private life with Maureen is the happiest time I've known. But I can't ever introduce her to my friends because I can't bear to be the man with the fat girlfriend.

Those for whom self-image is important food for the soul stay in poor jobs with glamorous companies, or in stifling professions with superior profiles, or in abysmal marriages to important people. What about you? Is an injury to your self-image part of the loss you will have to tolerate if you leave your comfort zone behind?

Certainly, self-image is not the only example of a potentially limiting belief. In Chapter Four we talked about the profoundly restrictive effects of the underlying negative assumption "I don't deserve better." Amy has struggled free from the shadow of this belief, a remnant from her early relationship with her dad. In a notable burst of courage, she undid some of its crippling effect in the process of divorcing her husband, challenging her insidious thinking by reminding herself: I deserve better, damn it. Or, deserve it or not, I'm going to try and get it.

Bursts of courage do not always have instant happy endings, and old limiting beliefs sprout again, tenacious weeds in our psychological gardens. The childhood belief that "I don't deserve better" has crept into Amy's relationship with her daughter, allowing Amy to tolerate disrespect and settle for rudeness. "I chose the divorce," she would think, "I can't blame my daughter for resenting me." Maternal guilt refueled Amy's early childhood assumptions. Temporarily they tied her to the miserable, martyred divorce tug-of-war.

Amy needed to weed-whack her old, familiar refrain "I don't deserve better." Once again she diminished the force of that negative idea by replacing it with a more accurate and constructive statement. "My daughter is entitled to be angry, but I am entitled to civility and respect. We each have our rights." This balanced and reasonable thought powered much of Amy's forward motion.

Replacement is often an effective strategy for letting go of limiting beliefs. You can't necessarily block the restrictive thought, but, like Amy, you can reshape it into a more productive force.

Remember Lydia, single and hoping for marriage and motherhood? Lydia had the fixed idea that single motherhood meant giving up on love forever. Essentially, she saw herself at a fork in her road. Her familiar, well-worn path said "Wait to find the guy and then have the baby"—sensible enough but unsuccessful to date, and time was running out. Her alternative path was marked "Give up on the guy and get the baby without him." After all, she reasoned, if no one loves me now, single and available, who will want me with the whiff of baby spit-up? Lydia believed that she could have a child, but at the bitter price of giving up on love. No wonder she was immobilized.

Lydia's limiting belief has no particular basis in reality. The fact is, women with children sometimes find new love and marriage; unencumbered women are sometimes isolated a lifetime. There are no guarantees, though what you believe probably affects your outcome. Lydia cut her ties to her comfort zone by replacing her limiting belief with a different version of her own future. We tried various renditions, but the one she liked best was "It's a long life, and not everything comes in the anticipated order. I'm going to reach for what I can and have faith that the rest will be delivered through the new doors I've forced open."

Ryan was able to rethink the sex appeal of the packaging plant once he discovered the utter cool of membership in something called The Executive's Association, a club for under-forty, upper-level executives of corporations, whose members try to do enough good to disguise the sheer thrill of being included in such rich company. Ryan's belief that "I'm too creative for boxes" became "Boxes are a vehicle. Success is the goal."

With the dazzling vision of qualifying for a club that was completely taken with itself, and not yet interested in taking him, Ryan began an all-out seduction campaign designed to woo his grandfather into someday soon bestowing an impressive management title on him. True, he has yet to tackle his procrastination or reduce his pot smoking. Still, letting go of his limiting belief that he was too good for his job freed Ryan to develop a new attitude toward work. I haven't seen such a turnaround since Anne Heche dumped Ellen.

Leaving her alcoholic lover was also easier for Frances after she disciplined her thinking. "I'm too old to start over" was replaced with "I'm too old to waste another minute." The truth of that restatement crept up on her slowly, increasing its impact with every repetition.

If you can identify your own limiting belief—*I don't deserve more; I'm too stupid/boring/fat/unattractive/unlucky/unlovable to get what I want*—recognize that these old negative assumptions are comfort zones in and of themselves and usually their own form of a trap. Leave them behind slowly by replacing each assumption with a different, more accurate, and more promising version of the issue. Replacement is a simple and hugely effective strategy. But it will require all your discipline and a commitment to structure to make it work for you.

Write down your negative, limiting thought so you are completely conscious of it. Then refine your replacement thought and write it down. Write it again. Write it a hundred times. Or a thousand. Silly as it seems, you can't write or say your new thought too often. Every repetition enhances its power.

Invoke a structure that helps you reinforce your replacement thought. Repeat it at every red light, or on every elevator ride, or whenever you sip something. Practice the new thought, repeat it inwardly over and over, tell it to other people as if you believed it. With practice, the new, less limiting version of your belief will become increasingly comfortable and then closer and closer to what's true for you. Remember, they are *your* thoughts. You are allowed to have them work on your behalf.

Who Am I Trying to Protect, and How Will My Progress Hurt That Person?

Reflecting on those you need to protect, you will probably first identify the people you will leave behind, or those you will uproot—the spouse who needs you though he couldn't satisfy you, the boss who trained you but can't pay you what some stranger will, the family from whom you are moving away, and worst, the children who will be affected whether you leave your comfort zone or hold on to it forever. We have already discussed these potent ties, forged by love, guilt, and obligation, which form the bulk of the adhesive in your current comfort zone.

There is a secondary group of people who also have a stake in your comfort zone, though they are less directly involved. Every one of them—parents, siblings, close friends, colleagues, neighbors—will feel the impact of your change, and their feelings affect you also.

For example, Marshall was first on Karin's list of guilty obligations. ("I don't want to be his wife, but I don't want to be his executioner either," she said.) Surprisingly, her parents' potential disappointment restricted Karin's choices almost as much. "My mom is finally planning a daughter's wedding after being mother-of-the-groom so many times. I can't do this to her," and "Underneath, I think my dad would be jealous of a man like Bob. I can't face Dad's disapproval."

Amy, too, continued to battle her ex as much to satisfy other people as herself. Certainly she believed she needed to protect her children as much as possible from their father's corrupting influence, but her own mother seemed as invested in the battle against Amy's ex-husband as Amy herself was. She wouldn't want Mom to think her weak.

What about you? Is someone else's pain your greatest obstacle to letting go? If so, how do you decide between yourself and someone you love?

First, get out of your head and put the issue on the table. Try to make a realistic assessment of what impact your choices will have on people you value. You can do that best by talking it over with them.

This conversation is appropriate in every case *except with your children when you are considering divorce*. There is great temptation to seek reassurance from the child that she will be "all right," a reassurance that no child can responsibly give, though many will try. It's natural to want such solace, but it's not appropriate to put that additional burden on a child. Comforting you is not your child's job.

With that one exception, you can approach the people whose feelings you are trying to protect and express your concerns directly. "Mom, I'm thinking about moving to California and I'm worried about how that move will affect you." "Dad, I'm not happy with law school and I'm thinking of dropping out. I know you'll be disappointed and your feelings are important to me. Can we talk about how my decision will affect you?"

Note that you are *not* asking for permission for your decision. Instead, you are using this conversation to acknowledge the impact of your choice on an important person, to let that person know you care about how he or she feels, and you will take those feelings into account when you make your decision. Just that respectful acknowledgment might ease not only your guilt but their pain.

The conversation could surprise you. Many people who put off divorce for a decade, firmly believing that a parent would be crushed by the sad news, discover that those same parents are unsurprised, even completely accepting, when confronted with the unpleasant reality. Likewise, mentors we dread disappointing may be more responsive than we imagined when notified of the possibility of a job change. You could come away from this talk with the kind of support that makes letting go so much easier.

Then again, you might not. Even if the talk is a dead end—the other person gets angry, insists on telling you what not to do, or flat out refuses to continue the conversation—you are still one step closer to letting go. *You've broken a boundary by airing the issue.* Passing that boundary edged you out of your comfort zone and into the field of anxiety you are required to cross. That's painful, but it's progress.

Suppose, worst case, that you discover your concerns are grounded in perfect truth: your mom's heart really would break if you filed for divorce, your dad really would have a stroke should you leave the family business, your older brother really would hate you forever if you made more money than he does. Does that mean that these needs, the frailties of those you love, will dictate the frame of your comfort zone forever?

Maybe. Maybe not. Only you can choose which of the needs of others you will assault or assuage. But you are helpless before the demands of others if you are unaware of your own needs. That is why you have looked back. That is why you have worked to create a vision, to understand what you would want for yourself, so it can weigh on the scales against what others want from you.

Karin owes something to her dad, to her mom, to Marshall. Amy surely owes consideration to her children and to her own mother's feelings. But what, how much, and how to balance the desires of others with your own conflicting ones?

The only balancing scale you can legitimately use are your personal values regarding obligation and integrity. If your measurement is conscious and frank, that scale will be enough.

I believe, for example, that the generation that will be injured by your choice is a significant variable in the decision. In my value system, we owe our children more than we owe our parents, and if there is any sacrificing to be done, the next generation is the proper direction for that sacrifice. According to those values, if you recognize that leaving your marriage will be a positive thing for you but hurtful for your children (which is, sadly, frequently the case), then I think it is perfectly legitimate, even morally correct, to sacrifice your self-interest for the well-being of your children, at least until their adulthood. If, on the other hand, leaving your marriage will be positive for you but painful for your parents, I think their feelings have a less legitimate claim on your decision making.

You might disagree. You might weigh your obligations to your elders far more heavily than those to your child, as many cultures do. Alternatively, you might value your personal happiness over the feelings of any other interested party. Certainly there is a whole school of self that would support this position.

Make your decision consciously, according to your personal values, and then stand to face the consequences of whichever path you choose. Denying these consequences is really the only way you can go wrong. The choice between ourselves and the people we care for is so tough, we sometimes pretend there is no choice at all.

Fathers leave their families, arguing that the children are better off without them. Mothers choose divorce, insisting the kids will be happier apart from Dad. Children move away from aging parents, assuring themselves that the sister left behind as caregiver was the favored child anyway. Professionals abandon or betray colleagues, insisting that the decision was "just business." We use every defense—rationalization, denial, blame, fantasy—to ignore the cost of our choices. The problem is, when we ignore those costs, we can't mitigate them at all.

When you are choosing between your own needs and the needs of a peer—whether it's a business partner you've outgrown, a sad sister who wishes you'd stay single, too, a close colleague who would resent your promotion, or a lover whose heart will break, as Karin fears that Marshall's will—the criteria for your decision are less clear. You have to weigh the value of that relationship to you and the nature of the promises you've made. You may have to decide between yourself and someone important to you, who is perhaps riding that dead horse, too.

As you make any of these difficult choices, keep your impulse to protect others in some kind of reasonable perspective. It's too easy to be carried away by the emotional drama of it all. Pain, after all, is not necessarily devastation. Sometimes it's only the shout of people who have been forced out of their own comfort zones.

For example, Amy might recognize her mom's anger without being completely guided by it. After all, Mom has had her chance to struggle with an ex-husband in her own way. It's Amy's turn now, and she's entitled to handle things differently. As for Amy protecting her children, closer examination showed that to be more of a wishful impulse than a real-life maternal obligation. Amy's children are adults, and her ongoing battle with their father does not protect them from him because they don't want that protection. Letting go of the competition with her ex will not hurt her kids or unjustly injure her own mother. It will be hard on Amy herself—what change isn't?—but ultimately the balm of being out of the battlefield will be the reward of letting go.

And what if Karin ripped off the Band-Aid of her engagement, let everyone moan for the time that they needed to, and then allowed the wounds to heal? Would her mother be disappointed? Yes, but Karin will probably eventually marry and there will be another wedding down the line. Will Dad disapprove? Probably. But Dad can't be the only one satisfied at the marriage. The bride has to have a smile on her face, too. Dad will have to get over it. He will, too. Karin's parents are resilient human beings and adults to boot. It's the fear of hurting them that is slowing Karin down. The hurt itself will pass.

What about Marshall? Will he be hurt? Certainly. Will he be destroyed, as she fears? Well, Karin had some recent experience practicing saying no to Marshall over smaller conflicts and that hadn't seemed to overwhelm him. Perhaps he was not as fragile or dependent as Karin imagined.

We began to talk about Marshall in a more three-dimensional way. Maybe he wasn't merely the simple Mr. Nice Guy foil for Karin's Bad Girl. Maybe Marshall was a person with issues and dynamics of his own. After all, hadn't he chosen to be engaged to an elusive, ambivalent woman? Did she think that was an accident, or did that maybe say something about Marshall? Why does Karin have to see him as a saint? Isn't he entitled to be as crazy as the rest of us?

Marshall might use a broken engagement to reevaluate choices, to nudge his own developing self-awareness, to struggle with his own issues regarding letting go. Or, he might blame his pain entirely on Karin's fickle heart and not look at himself at all. If that is the case, there will be nothing Karin can do about it. We all confront our own pathless path and make our own choices about whether to face forward or turn away.

In any event, extending an ambivalent engagement will not protect Marshall from pain. And certainly a faithless marriage would do him even more damage. Karin sees this truth, bites down on it, returns to her own sense of loss. What if this is all a mistake on her part? She is not in love with Marshall, true, but surely she loves him. Why isn't that enough? He is her opportunity for a normal life. Any other woman would want him. Shouldn't she hang on to him?

Karin's return to self-interest brings us to question three.

What Makes Letting Go Easier?

This is the jackpot question. Contemplate letting go and the painful threat looms before you as clearly as the Ghost of Christmas Future. You see it—the guaranteed salary vanishing, the old job savored by someone else, the discarded lover annoyingly happy in a new relationship—and it stops you in your tracks. What can you do to propel yourself forward?

First, *keep your eyes on the prize.* Remember, we choose loss only because we believe we stand to gain, and for no other reason. Invoke the vision you've put so much effort into. See it, say it, write it, visualize it, meditate on it, swear by it.

Next, *arm your inner voice* with all the tools it needs to counter your self-defeating thoughts. Letting go is a guerrilla skirmish fought inside your own head. You can win, you will win, but only if you deliberately arm the voice inside your head that's arguing for letting go. Otherwise your inner life is a never-ending Vietnam War, with constant painful clamor and a few hard-won, wounding victories but eventual hopeless, humiliating defeat.

The problem is, your comfort trap has a claim on you. You are attached to it—emotionally, intellectually, socially, financially. These attachments are real, they are visceral. And they have a voice. It is the voice of dread, restriction, guilt, affection, obligation, and habit. It is the soothing voice of what is comfortable and safe. It is the angry voice of all the people you love, who insist that you stay where you are so they can stay where they are. It is the internalized voice of your fearful father or your harsh mother. It is the cranky voice of your childhood, tantruming over any loss simply because it hurts.

Together, these voices form an internal chorus that swells at the very prospect of letting go. "I can't . . . It's not fair . . . I shouldn't have to . . . Not yet . . . There's no point trying . . . I'll do it tomorrow . . . It doesn't matter anyway . . . Just one more time . . . What if . . . Don't make me." This negative symphony of your current comfort zone insists you stay put. You need to be prepared to drown it out with a rousing forward march.

Thought-stopping helps. Catch yourself in a full round of fear-tripping, snap a rubber band at your wrist hard enough to get your attention, and then inwardly scream *Stop!* Combine that thought-stopping with positive substitutions—realistic thoughts that frame your choices in a positive direction.

We've talked about these replacement thoughts earlier in this chapter. Simply stated, every time you catch yourself in the act of thinking your paralyzing thought—"If I leave I'll be alone forever," "No one else would hire me," "It's too late," "I'm too old"—rehearse a concrete, positive thought to replace it.

Beyond that specific thought substitution, arm your inner voice by creating a short, pointed coaching script that strengthens your resolve and keeps you focused on letting go. Recovering alcoholics and addicts remind themselves "one day at a time." Ex-smokers combat the urge by repeating "I am not a smoker." Overeaters resist binges, thinking "Nothing tastes as good as thin and healthy feels." Women screw up their courage to leave abusive lovers, believing "Someone else will love me if I give myself a chance."

Write yourself one heartfelt statement that soothes your own fear or contradicts your own limiting belief. Once you have it, I repeat: Say it, write it, meditate on it, visualize it, swear by it. It will work.

When you are working on letting go, *welcome anger.* It's the time-honored grease of separation, and it helps. Emotional attachments are complicated beasts and so we feel many different ways about the same important people. We love and resent them, feel frustration and compassion often in equal doses. In Chapter Four we talked about how this natural emotional ambivalence is an obstacle to creating a singularly motivating vision. But when it comes to letting go, that ambivalence can be an ally. Somewhere buried in the pain of your prospective loss is some angry wish to break free. Find that anger.

Teenagers call on it to ease their passage from the shelter of parental arms. Employees focus on their frustrations to make leaving familiar work turf more palatable. Mates fuel their separations by stoking their rage and suppressing their affection. If you can get mad at the people who are holding you in place, that anger will act as an anesthetic against the pain of losing them when you let go.

Finally, *let go in small, tolerable steps.* Each one—the cigarette you did not smoke, the phone call you resisted returning, the résumé finally revised—influences your ability to let go further, minutely reshaping your view of yourself as the person who will leave her current comfort zone and establish a fresh beachhead.

Every time Amy refuses to please her capricious daughter, she establishes herself as a less mouselike presence in her own mind. Every productive hour Ryan spends at his office makes the possibility of his establishing an adult professional identity inside that business more feasible to him. When Diane developed a friendship with a college student, she was more able to identify herself as a potential college student. If Lydia finally consults an adoption specialist, just that person's matter-of-fact willingness to talk with her would probably loosen her belief that she must be married before she becomes a mother.

If you take a small step in the direction you might want to go—accept a date even though you can't let go of your bad boyfriend, take a management night course even though you can't picture yourself leaving your stressful sales job, take ice skating lessons even though you can't envision yourself losing the thirty pounds—these modest changes can have a huge impact on your ability to let go. What they can do, in effect, is change what you envision.

Change your vision and you will feed your ability to take small steps in a new direction. As you take those small steps, the process of letting go has begun. You have momentum. Think of letting go as cutting your moorings. Yes, it will involve a loss. But it will give you liftoff.

From that aerial perspective the fears you have dreaded to face will shrink to a more reasonable scale. And you will finally be able to face them down.

CHAPTER 8

BREAK THE COMFORT BARRIER

Y ou will always be given the same advice. It will always be true. That will never make it any easier to take.

The advice? Simple: Act. Seize the moment. Take the risk. Make the effort. Take on the struggle. Try something new. Just do it. All excellent strategies for living. Each requiring monumental effort, though sometimes only for an instant.

That effort is the rock push we talked about in Chapter One. This is its last grunting shove to the top of the hill. Make the push over the top toward the vision you have refined, and you stand a good chance of tumbling down to land in that newer, happier place.

So close to the top, though, you might still back away because of what you are pushing against. Your last obstacle is fear and you will have to face it down.

To this point you have established your new direction,

loosened your ties to your familiar comfort trap, and decided the time to act is now. But you cannot get from here to where you want to go without crossing the fire walk of anxiety. Every comfort zone is surrounded by it, whether roaring or merely a rosy threat.

You have to walk over the coals. But you don't have to go barefoot.

The Barrier of Dread

Step six: Face Your Fear finds you at the very doorway to your anxiety. Take that one step, do that one uncomfortable thing, and you will be out the door and right in the middle of your tightrope. You have been thinking, analyzing, processing. Now you need to act.

Go ahead, you are coaching yourself, do it—say "I quit" or walk in and argue for your raise, give back the ring or get down on your knees and hand one over, put your portfolio in front of the gallery owner, agree to take on the chairmanship, register for the class that might make you look foolish, join the group where you don't know anyone. Get out of your comfort zone and get on with your life.

You are poised to make progress, facing forward, urging yourself on, when . . . a feeling stops you dead. It's only a feeling, but for the moment it might as well be a wall. That feeling is fear, though it presents itself in many masks.

To get past that fear, first you have to recognize it. Your fear response to a physical threat is the most familiar, with its universal heart-thudding, gut-clutching, breath-shortening fight-or-flight response. But your reaction to an emotional risk will be far more varied and disguised. You may have to learn to identify fear buried beneath your repertoire of dodgy moves and distractions.

The fear you'll need to push through runs the spectrum from mere reluctance to downright horror. Surprisingly, there's no pure correspondence between the intensity of your feeling and the likelihood of your action. Simple hesitation may hold you back longer than gulping panic, depending on how many techniques you use to urge yourself into the unknown and how effective they are.

Some of us chant our fear in the worried mantra "what if . . . what if . . . what if . . ." Others mask it with presentable excuses— "I can't because . . ." or "I'm waiting until . . ."—and so they may miss their underlying anxiety entirely. You could be in the full, stomach-churning, pincer grip of your fear, vowing repeatedly to take your risk—but tomorrow, tomorrow, tomorrow. Or you may be oblivious, completely preoccupied with rearranging the furniture in your own safe tower. Whether you are completely self-aware or unconscious, fear will be a factor when you take that step into discomfort.

For some, the barrier of anxiety surrounding a comfort zone is a sharp sliver of feeling, an acute dread of only a brief encounter and its consequences. Karin, for example, envisions Bob's wrath and Marshall's pain when she tells each that she's leaving. Her fear of facing their reactions is so great that she can't bring herself to make her announcement. Yet everything would be instantly different if she acted.

Or, your fear might be a thick soupy fog of uncertainty. Ryan's familiar role of family screwup has run out of juice, but suiting up for a more satisfying part, one that will win him his club invitation, will require risky action. Should he go to business school? (But what if he can't get in? What if it's the most boring thing on earth? What if he flunks out?) Why not get a friend to help him write a business plan and present it to the family? (But what if he can't answer their questions? What if they laugh at him or dismiss him?) None of his fears is fully defined. All of them chorus to keep him in place.

Your own fear may be an intimidating acquaintance whose power is long known and completely accepted. When Ruth lost all that weight and then fled back to the companionship of food and television after only one date, she was disappointed in herself but not surprised. "I think I'm like a car accident victim who never drives again," she said. "I just can't take the possibility of another crash." Ruth has become resigned to her fear of rejection and so her comfort zone feels permanent.

Amy's fear, on the other hand, is new to her because she's working at the very edges of her comfort zone. Amy has con-ceived the idea of taking a Christmas trip, thereby sitting out the annual family drama regarding how her kids will divide their time between their parents. But her kids firmly frown on Amy's independent plans. Amy's daughter got in a dig that "at least Dad doesn't abandon us at a family time of year."

Amy fell so firmly into a mud bath of guilt it was tough to see through to the fear beneath. But it was there: the worrisome thought that if she takes care of herself, her children will resent her and grow farther away from her. After all, her children's love means far more than any vacation ever could. Why risk their wrath? The potential consequences are too scary.

Sometimes a long path is studded with fear, progress made only by pushing past each emotional boulder. After her soul-searching conversations with God, Lydia had diminished her fears of becoming a single mother, at least sufficiently to proceed with the complicated choices of adoption agency, financial planning, relocation. Her fear did not evaporate, certainly. At each new step—explaining her decision to key people at work, revealing her intentions to her parents, telling a new man about her future plans, evaluating countries for possible adoption—fear made her hesitate, procrastinate, and second-guess herself. In theory she is resolute in her procession from the comfort zone of her cozy job and creative hobby to her new niche as unmarried mom. In fact, for every two steps forward, fear drags her under the covers for a while. The question is, What gets her out?

And will it work for you?

It's one thing to say "just do it," but the fact is there are many strategies that will make doing it far more likely. This is the moment when you call on everything you've learned about challenging your comfort zone. In the end, you will still have to step off the curb and into traffic. You can, however, make that a safe, smart, and confident step.

What follows from here is a reprise of everything we've talked about, focused pointedly on the ever-present and last lingering barrier to change: fear itself.

Fear Itself

Whatever the object of your fear, remember this: *The fear itself resides in you. And that means you can manage it.*

This idea is so important, it bears repeating. Whatever you fear—the disapproval of your parents though you are pushing forty, the interview you will surely mishandle, the spouse who snarls at your slightest resistance, the lover who will scorn you if you ask for more, the wrong decision that will result in financial upheaval or missed opportunity—your obstacle is *not* that person, that problem, that decision. Your obstacle is the fear itself, and that fear belongs to you.

Surely "we have nothing to fear but fear itself" ranks up there with the great psychological truisms. Like so many adages, these observations are self-evident until we apply them to ourselves, at which point they become surprisingly elusive. Recognizing that it is fear itself that is your obstacle, and not the focus of the fear, is tough to do when you're in the middle of it.

It seems to Karin that Bob's anger is her problem, or Marshall's painful dependence, or both. But her obstacle is neither of these; it's Karin's fear of them that is holding her back.

Ruth assumes that her weight is her obstacle, or her food dependency or her reliable attraction to mean men. None of these adds much to her life, but they are not her barrier. It's her fear that is barring her way; her weight, her overeating, her self-criticism merely serve to support that fear.

You are afraid of something or someone, too, and you have probably paid that something or someone far too much attention already. Now turn your attention to yourself, to the fear itself. That's the voice that's making your decisions. That's the voice you need to drown.

That voice is screaming *Stop!*

Consider any stretch beyond the boundaries of your comfort zone, and you will receive your personal fear signal, whether it is a swamp of confusion, a paralyzing wash of sadness, or the too-familiar stomach stab of dread. Regardless of whether your fear is well-camouflaged or undisguised anguish, its message is always the same: *Stop where you are! You are moving into uncomfortable territory.*

Get the message and you will stop, you must stop, at least for a while. You will stop until you learn when and how to override that message. Now the question is: How do you force yourself to proceed through a psychological stop sign?

- By facing the fact that there's a price for inaction— it hurts where you are. (Face What Hurts)
- By evaluating the risks carefully and measuring those risks against the positive vision you've created. (Create a Vision)
- By deciding that now is the time to take those risks. (Make a Decision)
- By identifying the source of those stop signals from your earlier experience. (Identify a Pattern)
- By recognizing and making peace with the losses those risks will probably entail. (Let Go)
- Finally, as we'll discuss in detail in this chapter, by proceeding forward to overcome your fear with energy, support, and a plan to maximize your chances for success. (Face Fear)

As you see, you've been pushing against your wall of fear all along. Each of the previous steps is, in itself, a gradual effort to whittle down fear bit by bit. That's why so many of the fear-fighting techniques we will discuss next were applicable to earlier stages in this process. Those techniques are particularly useful now, when fear is a more naked foe.

In the end, though, those first several steps we've discussed will not be enough to free you from your comfort zone entirely. Cementing your progress will come down to a moment, more likely a series of moments, when you will either act or not act. The likelihood of your action will depend, in the end, on how you manage fear.

Think of fear as a distinct entity inside you. It exists in the form of ideas, emotions, and physical sensations. You will exorcise fear through these same three channels: redirecting your thoughts; quieting your troubled feelings and easing your physical discomfort; and taking the active steps that put fear behind you and push your rock over the top.

Here's the bottom line: Fear only goes away when you do the thing you're afraid of. That's true for two reasons. First, because you got the thing done, so it's not looming anymore. Second, because you have demonstrated to yourself that, whatever the consequences of your much-feared action, you can handle them.

This last is especially important. Psychologist Susan Jeffers, who has succinctly distilled the conventional wisdom on fear in *Feel the Fear and Do It Anyway*, makes this point again and again. No matter what the specific issue on which your fear has chosen to focus itself, all fear has one underlying emotional message, namely, "I'm afraid I can't handle it." Action is the antidote to this insidious thought.

Having said that you need to take action, the other truth is that there are a host of things you can do, actually probably must do, in order to get yourself to take that scary step. There are strategies that will make you more likely to break through your anxiety and make it to the new comfort zone toward which you are aiming.

As we discussed in Chapter Six, your smartest first step forward might be a look back or a step inside. What you are looking for this time is the most productive, most motivating way to understand your fear. That's thinking you can use to break through your comfort barrier.

Formulating Fear

Fear, in particular, urges us to ascribe magical power to our ability to answer the *why* question. That's partly because the longer we wonder why we are afraid, the longer we can delay facing that particular fear. But we linger on *why* for another, more compelling reason. Fear can seize us so irrationally that we feel powerless before its mysterious tides. Intuitively, we feel that if we could make sense of that fear, it would be a step toward mastering it. To some extent, that turns out to be true.

Fear first draws your attention to the question "What am I afraid of, and why?" Begin to answer by looking back to locate the original source of today's fear. Sometimes the answer is obvious; other times you can make a good guess. Either answer might be useful in reducing today's fear.

Lydia, for example, knows she's scared to reveal her parenting plans to her parents; they've always been harshly disapproving of any step off a tried-and-true path. She anticipates the same verbal slap this time around and she's scared to confront it. Or, you might make a more general psychological link between your past experience and present fear, as Lydia did when she realized that her supervisor was a kind of surrogate parent, and she feared telling him about the time off she needed because she anticipated a similar lack of support.

Again, understanding the link between today's fearful reactions and old emotional freight can help you to separate past and present. It's easier to muster your courage to face a current threat when you are not confusing it with the old bogeymen from your childhood. As we discussed in Chapter Six, identify that mental association and then remind yourself, quite deliberately, that the situation you now face is not identical. This boss is not your dad. This social group is not the one that shunned you in the fifth grade. This colleague is not your prettier sister. You don't have to bring that old discomfort with you. Such distinct separation of past anxiety and present challenge helps to reduce fear. In this situation, knowing "why" helps.

It helps to have a theory about why you are afraid, but it's not essential. The most effective way for analysis to help you master a current fear is to identify the fear as part of a personal developmental theme. Once you identify the pattern that links your risky action to a developmental theme, you increase your motivation to take that action, scary though it is.

Start by categorizing your fear around a more general personal issue. These categories of fear are fairly standard:

- Fear of rejection—"I can't risk the contest because I can't bear not being chosen."
- Fear of commitment—"I can't choose, decide, close the door, because I might make a mistake or miss an opportunity."
- Fear of separation—"I can't bear to be without him/her. Anything is better than being alone."
- Fear of intimacy—"I can't reveal myself because I won't be loved."
- Fear of confrontation—"I can't face the pain of displeasure."
- Fear of being controlled—"I don't want to be taken advantage of. I can't submit to another's will."

There is no one way to make this list, and surely many categories overlap. Confrontation, for example, usually raises the threat of rejection; rejection triggers the possibility of painful separation; fear of intimacy and a concern about being controlled generally go hand in hand. The point is to generalize your current fear to whichever larger category you feel applies for the purpose of focusing your energy on overcoming that fear.

It is easier to force yourself to talk to the colleague who took credit for your idea if you are on a mission to overcome your fear of confrontation. Otherwise you are apt to rationalize your avoidance, reasoning that this colleague is impossible to talk to, this idea wasn't that important, and so on.

You are more likely to take on a high-risk job if you have identified yourself as being limited by your fear of failure. Without that generalization you might talk yourself out of that opportunity, oblivious to the fear that is fueling your reasons.

You are more likely to challenge your sexual comfort zone if you recognize that your reluctance to experiment is founded on a fear of intimacy. A conscious desire to come closer to love makes you sexually braver.

Look within yourself to categorize your fear because that will increase your motivation to break your own comfort barrier.

Analyzing the *what* and *why* of your fear can both reduce it to more tolerable size and inspire you to confront it, but it will never erase the fear entirely. That can only be done through *direct action*.

Recall that Karin recognized the connection between her dread of disappointing Bob and the helplessness she felt as a little girl confronting a majestically disapproving dad. Her recognition certainly took some of the edge off her fear, consciously allowing her to distinguish her adult relationship with Bob from her natural childhood impotence vis-à-vis her father. That distinction makes Bob's anger easier to confront. But it will still be a risk and Karin will still be afraid, until she faces Bob's anger and survives it.

Likewise, when Amy identified the pattern of self-effacement that made insisting on her rights with her own kids more difficult, it increased Amy's motivation to confront that anxiety. It did not, however, entirely erase it. Only surviving the discomfort of asserting herself can do that.

Merely recognizing her long-standing separation anxieties will not be sufficient to make Frances leave her alcoholic lover. She will also need the courage to endure the lash of loneliness for as long as it lasts.

Ryan came to think of his professional halfheartedness as a reflection of his own fears of failure and reluctance to commit to an adult identity. These psychological formulations focused his obstacles back inside himself, rather than on the limitations of the box business or the personality problems of his grandfather. He began to see himself as less a victim of his situation and more the source of his own difficulties. That meant it was in his power to make his life better. But that improvement would require action. The thought of action, past the boundary of what is comfortable, inspires fear.

Prudent analysis of the reasons for your fear can be salve for past pain and inspiration for future risk. The risk, though, is unavoidable. You have to walk the tightrope, but you can do it with a net.

Walking the Tightrope

This whole book has been about facing fear, about inching out onto a tightrope toward that next unknown platform. When we feel afraid, we snuggle into what is at least comfortably safe, simultaneously avoiding pain while imagining just how torturous that pain would be. To escape your comfort trap you will need to reverse that process. Instead of snuggling down, you will need to step out actively. Instead of elaborating on the fearful possibilities, you will need to think thoughts that will minimize the fear and maximize your strength.

In every chapter thus far I have described techniques that will help you do just that. We started with Jack, whose fear of making a mistake by marrying Jane prevented him from moving forward, while his fear of separation and loss prevented him from letting her go. Over time, and through conversation with me and with his friends, Jack applied the universal balms for fear.

First, he got a clear picture of what he wanted (remember the Couple in the Black Mercedes?) and separated it deliberately, consciously, and repeatedly from what he feared. It's so easy to mush together your hopes and doubts into one big stew, letting anxiety water down the strength of your vision. Jack kept his vision clear, mentally focusing on his icon of happily ever after. He bundled his fears in a list of what-ifs and viewed them as luggage strapped to the back of his Mercedes.

Next, Jack used a series of mental tricks to reduce the weight of this bundle. He challenged his negative thoughts, objectively restating them so they were less debilitating to him. For example, "What if I lose my assets in a divorce?" became "What if marriage puts me in a stronger financial position?" "What if she's the wrong person?" was restated as "What if she's my soul mate and I lose her because I'm too scared?" Every negative thought can be challenged and restated in a more productive way, though Jack, and you, must consciously focus on making that restatement. It won't just happen automatically.

Finally, Jack made a plan to test marriage by living together; as he worked hard to encourage Jane to go along with the plan, he persuaded himself as well. Action overcame the anxiety that swamped Jack earlier when he did nothing but sit around and study his palms. (On the one hand . . . but then, on the other . . .)

Those same four elements:

- Outside support—whether friend, mentor, or professional—to bolster your strength
- A goal, a hope, a reason, a reward—held clearly in your mind's eye as distinctly separate from all your doubts about it or fears of it
- A program of cognitive and relaxation techniques aimed specifically at minimizing those fears and doubts
- A structured plan of action, so you can put one foot in front of the other, moving toward your vision regardless of the ebb and flow of those fears

will carry you to your next, higher platform.

Get Support

"The tongue is the best masseur for a troubled brow" is wisdom attributable either to the ancient Sufis or to very modern Internet pundits. Either way it's smart advice to keep in mind. The fact is, expressing your fears to a supportive person goes a long way toward actually easing your burden.

You cannot overstate the power of relationship in overcoming fear. Fear weakens us, but courage can be borrowed, strength shared. Anxiety clouds everyone's vision, but a loving parent, an informed colleague, a caring spouse, a knowing friend can pierce that cloud.

Of course, close relationships may be just as likely to maximize your fear as to reduce it. For one thing, the people who are closest to us have a stake in our staying the same, fulfilling their same needs, maintaining the comfort zones we share with them. Conflict of interest can make those closest to us reluctant to encourage us in a major change—relocation, career shift, marriage, divorce—because the impact on them is too painful.

Also, the people closest to us identify with us, and so often feel similarly afraid or reluctant. "He only leads who goes before," and if a confidant has not overcome a similar risk in his own life, he may not have the courage available for inspiration.

But these are the obstacles, and the rewards of support are so vast it's worth seeking despite its imperfections. Not every friendship or family relationship will offer unconditional support, but you can return again and again to those who will. You need to talk to someone who is not frightened by your fear, who sees past the difficult moment to the possibility of a positive outcome, who encourages you to go toward that future.

That somebody might be a professional, as it was for Jack and the other people you've read about here. In only a few instances was I their only source of support. Most had a variety of confidants who offered the brew of advice, alarm, encouragement, and admonition common to supportive friendships.

There are several advantages, though, to adding the support of a psychotherapist to this assemblage. For one thing, unlike a friend, a professional can be completely committed to supporting the part of you that wants to change, even when you don't know for some time what that change will look like. The professional distance between you means that the therapist's life is not affected by your decision, so she can focus more objectively on your agenda. And because she's being paid for just such a purpose, she has more permission to press, confront, and nudge you forward than your mother does. Not that much more permission, but some.

Support in the form of a peer group—AA, for example, or any diet or stop-smoking group—is also a powerful fear weapon. Other participants know your fear firsthand, and are quick to see it hiding beneath your rationalizations. They build courage, loan strength, reinforce vision, and supply structure. An hour in their presence is invigorating, even if you choose not to speak.

But speak. *The tongue is the best masseur for a troubled brow.*

Keep Your Eyes on the Prize

Remember that *vision is the ability to see something that does not yet exist.* Therefore the vision toward which you are moving might be the merest shadow, a glimmer of an idea, a wish. Yes, it's better, easier, more motivating to have a precise goal. Hell, having ten goals and a five-year plan, plus the talent and passion to fuel your pursuit, is best of all. But it's not required.

Sometimes in life we challenge a comfort zone simply for the sake of movement, to stir things, to breathe fresh air, with no idea of where we will land—and that's fine, too. To keep your eyes on the prize successfully, all you need is a flicker of a positive idea, a faint thought of some possible gain, just enough wisp of vision to risk that first, if reluctant, step.

When you challenge your comfort zone the actual rewards reaped might be unexpected. One woman reflected on the surprising payoff of her divorce: "All the tension in my own family visits vanished when my marriage did. My ex never wanted to be there, never wanted to participate. He'd always go off to some other room to watch sports or make a phone call. And that made me tense and furious with him and not very good company for everybody else. Now I'm relaxed, my folks enjoy my visits more. Oddly enough, I lost a husband, but I seem to have regained a father." You, too, may be unable realistically to envision all the good that will come from your stretch. Like this woman, you won't need to. Stretch, and be surprised.

Remember, too, that the prize you envision might be, and so often is, an internal one. Jack moved more determinedly toward commitment because he understood that he had always avoided it and he wanted to be strong enough to face his fear of closing a door. Karin practiced saying no to men for the same reason. She had no real image of how her relationships with men would improve if she added "no" to her repertoire along with her perennial "yes"; she just wanted the courage to be and do more than she was. Personal challenge can be vision enough to inspire you to face fear, emphasizing a way you want to *be* rather than on a goal you want to achieve.

There are emotional achievements, of course. And they are priceless. Face a fear for no greater reason than that you have identified that fear and don't want it to stand in your way anymore, and you are moving toward a better version of yourself. Your resulting feelings are predictable. The slippery prize of self-esteem, which so many rue as absent from their childhoods, is freely accessible to the adult who deliberately faces a fear. The resulting light in your soul, the feeling of pride, the easing of your ordinary quavering angst, may all be banked for the moment when a more concrete goal appears.

And now that you see you're the kind of person who is brave and worthy of more, you can allow that more concrete vision to appear. And so the loop continues. Those who stretch improve their capacity to stretch more, to see more toward which to reach, and so to improve their grasp.

The rest stay put.

Replace Fearful Thoughts

Fear, in all its forms, is so emotionally compelling that we give it way too much airtime. We embroider our fearful thoughts, elaborate on our mental pictures of tormenting outcomes, lavishly indulge our worst ideas. Then we broadcast an endless loop of what-ifs and I don't wannas on a twenty-four-hour brain cable channel. The fact is, you can change your broadcast.

Techniques for diminishing the power of your negative thoughts are almost stupidly simple. In effect, you just have to force yourself, resolutely, to think something else.

Try not to let the simplicity of this idea put you off. It works as well on you and on me as it works on your cocker spaniel. Mention to your dog that he's a "good boy" and he feels good. Doesn't matter whether it's the twentieth time you've told him today. He still wags his tail. Tell yourself "good girl" in all the complicated ways you might do that, and you know what? Something inside you will wag its tail, too. You'll sit up straighter, feel braver, try harder. No matter how many times you send yourself some version of that positive thought, it will work every time.

But you'll have to actually do it. Somehow, fear thoughts need no help. Reach the edge of your comfort zone, if only in your mind's eye, and automatically you will start broadcasting fear, dread, worry, and weakness. Challenging those fear thoughts, though, requires conscious effort. It has to be done deliberately, repeatedly, even religiously.

We've reviewed different versions of this thought replacement technique in several earlier chapters—for example, writing a script to coach yourself through avoidance, or arming your inner voice with challenging thoughts to give you the strength to let go. Use a variation of those techniques now to diminish your incapacitating negative thoughts.

First, become as conscious of your negative thoughts as you possibly can. Even though they flow in a constant mental stream, they are often background noise, eroding your courage in an inaudible mumble of misery. Bring that mumble to high volume. Picture the risky step you might take and then ask yourself, "What is it I'm trying to avoid?" or "What am I afraid of?"

Jack's bundle, if you'll recall, included his fear of making a mistake, of losing his financial independence, of being congenitally unfaithful and therefore a callous cad. Look back at Jack's story in Chapter Two for a vivid example of how every negative thought can be objectively restated in a more positive, less fearful way. The same kind of cognitive reshaping will minimize your own fears if you take the time to sit down, rewrite your thoughts, and then practice the new ones.

As Lydia contemplated single adoption, she included in her list of fears everything from her belief that no man would want her if she had a child, through her financial concerns, professional worries, social pressures, right down to the nagging concern that if she made her small den into a nursery she would have no place to put her TV. Next, she challenged every fearful thought with a plausible positive statement. "No man will want me with a child" became "I'll be able to relax into a relationship without my clock ticking so loud in my head." "I'll never handle a promotion with a child" became "Plenty of women manage careers and children. It's not perfect, but it doesn't have to be." Then she had the TV installed in a corner of her bedroom ceiling, decided she liked it even better there, and scheduled another session with the adoption counselor. Eighteen (long) months later she was the mother of Brazilian twins.

Not everyone can list her negative thoughts in such a concise fashion. Your experience might be closer to Karin's. Ask her why she so dreads her confrontations with either Bob or Marshall and she's the first to acknowledge that there's nothing rational to be afraid of. "Yes, they'll be very angry with me. Maybe mean things will be said, but it's just anger. Nothing to account for how I can't breathe when I imagine doing it."

It could be that your fear, like Karin's, is just that—a dread of those noxious physical reactions that are stirred in you for who-knows-what reason. What you avoid most might be the physical discomfort of your own fear.

Remember the neighbor whose thoughtlessly placed trash can was such an irritant in Chapter Three? For some, the worst part of making that awkward phone call is the unpleasant racing heart that would accompany the dialing of the phone, that god-awful anxiety that attends every confrontation and must be endured if you're going to act.

We feel these physical responses to our fears for "no reason," or no reason that makes sense to us. When Karin contemplates confrontation she gets a throat lump and chest pounding so toxic she instantly avoids the fearful act to get rid of the feeling. Frances, picturing separation from her alcoholic boyfriend, is similarly incapacitated. She conjures being alone, and wakes with a bleak, agitated nausea so acute that, on occasion, Frances has reconciled with her lover just to put herself out of her misery.

Who knows the source of such unpleasant arousal—why commitment triggers a sweaty panic in one person, while the possibility of rejection overwhelms another with premonitory grief? Perhaps an early childhood experience, coupled with an especially sensitive sympathetic discharge system, accounts for these physical reactions. Maybe there are some specific negative thoughts that trigger these reactions, ideas floating too far below consciousness to lasso and challenge.

Even in the absence of specific negative thoughts with which to work, you can reduce the physical effects of fear and anxiety and bring these unpleasant feelings to a tolerable level. Experiment with the yoga breathing (four breaths in through your nose and one breath out through the mouth) that we discussed in Chapter Five. Try relaxation techniques. Consider a short course of antianxiety medication if no less-dramatic method makes your fear level tolerable.

Don't ignore these physical miseries that accompany your anxious choices. They have too much power, forcing you back into bad situations or away from positive risks by dint of their sheer unpleasantness. Instead, do whatever you must—meditate, medicate, exercise—to reduce the toxic edge of your fear sufficiently to allow you to act.

Just don't lie there and do nothing. Fear must be fought, determinedly and actively. When you do fight it, you'll find it a surprisingly weak adversary. But it will not vanish on its own.

Take Action

Facing fear means overcoming avoidance, and so the action principles are identical with those we discussed in Chapter Three. Get yourself to act by identifying some specific next step and then applying the strictures of discipline and structure. A commitment to the teeth-gritting values of discipline, supported by a pragmatic, detailed plan of action, will get you across almost any anxious tightrope walk.

Recall the principles of discipline: Do the hard stuff first, be guided more by your head than your heart, decide to act now, and take any step in the right direction. Review the idea of structure — the commitment, planning, and execution of disciplined action, toward the goal, out in the middle of fear.

There's the theory. In the next chapter you'll see how differently it plays out in life.

CHAPTER 9

PRAY TO GOD
AND ROW TO SHORE

Seven steps out of your comfort zone are universal. Every person's passage, though, is individual.

The difference I have noticed in Karin is that her stories no longer portray her as an actor in a play in which someone else wrote the script. She has relinquished her childlike view that life happens to her. Karin will now describe an event, saying "I decided . . ." or "What I wanted . . ." or, even more perceptively, "It wasn't what I wanted but I went along because . . ." or, better yet, "What I could have done was . . ."

These are simple shifts in her perception, but simple change is usually all that is ever necessary. Simple change. Small steps. Big doors turn on small hinges. Every cliché a truth. Every truth tough to make a reality, when you are the person pushing against fear to make a change.

It had long been clear that Karin had to end her relationship with Bob. He was married, he was staying married, and that alone made the relationship a dead end. But was there a right way, a better way to end things that might keep Bob from being too offended? He was, after all, a partner in her firm. Wouldn't it be wise to maintain a cordial relationship with him, if only in the interests of job security?

Karin became absorbed in the how-to of confronting Bob, fantasizing that a perfect separation would mean a painless one for both of them. She fixed on the idea of sending Bob an e-mail that would explain her need to "cool things for the time being." She planned to describe herself as "confused," "needing time to sort out my feelings." She brought in a draft of this message for my comments. I pointed out that we knew she was afraid to close the door with Bob and this e-mail looked to me like she was leaving the door wide open. She missed her next session.

Eventually, in a brave impulse, Karin did send a similar e-mail to Bob, suggesting they stop meeting "for a while." Then she held her breath, bowed her head, and waited for the storm to break.

No storm came. Bob never acknowledged the e-mail, nor did he ever pursue a private relationship with her again. When they crossed paths, he offered Karin the exact bland, professionally pleasant mask he had always worn in the office, absent only the earlier private twinkle. It was over.

Karin was relieved and sad and fairly shocked at his complete and seamless role shift. Poof. All that passion, all that angst gone at the press of Send. Their relationship today is all civil business chatter, without even an undercurrent of past pleasure.

This week Karin took off Marshall's ring. She is waiting for him to notice, and when he does, she plans to give the ring back to him. It's an imperfect plan to be sure, because Marshall tends to avoid noticing and Karin is still so ambivalent about giving him up entirely. But she met a new man at a convention last week. They appear to be in the first shadowboxing stages of a courtship, and early signs suggest that he is a single Dr. Bob — smart, arrogant, elitist, successful, demanding, and sexy. I believe she's strong enough now to connect with this new dad as an equal. He's certainly who and what she wants. With her focus, drive, and courage, Karin will probably get it.

Perhaps there will continue to be many men for Karin; perhaps this latest romance will turn out to be *the* one. But she is a different woman now, more integrated, more whole. At least that's how it seems to me when I sit with her these days. Karin still wants to please men and she is a master of the pleasing arts. But now she wants to be pleased in return, can identify what she wants and needs, and can even reconcile a conflict between her own desires and a man's in her own favor from time to time.

The victories may appear small — Karin honoring her own movie preference, allowing herself honest sexual expression, refusing to apologize automatically when something is not her fault. But altogether, they indicate the ripening of a *self*, an autonomous, self-respecting, loving person. Karin has reached a new level of comfort with herself, and all her relationships will reflect the fact that she is operating from that new comfort zone. She took all the emotional risks necessary to get herself there and she deserves every bit of the reward.

Ryan is still smoking pot, still struggling against his grandfather's regime, still resisting paperwork as vigorously as his own three-year-old fights naptime. But he survived an evening school sales and accounting certification course that turned out to be less tedious than he'd always assumed. To his surprise, unlike in his family business environment, his classmates appeared to respect him and sought his input.

This unaccustomed support and approval have increased Ryan's enthusiasm for pursuing a business school program. Right now he takes an evening course once a week and he has no commitment to a degree. But he does take every opportunity to use his family business as a case study, and particularly to learn enough jargon and business basics to develop his expansion ideas with sound reality.

We've been working specifically on Ryan's cranky reluctance to face his desk, with the papers, projects, and tasks that he is required to complete in exchange for his paycheck. All good intentions aside, Ryan would interrupt any activity to take a phone call, schmooze with an office mate, or fiddle with his computer. He and I have introduced several techniques to put into operation the structure and discipline necessary to overcome his reluctance.

Simple methods have helped. He resolutely closes his office door and refuses phone calls for the first work hour of every day. Yes, it's uncomfortable behind that door. But hey, you're out of your comfort zone. Eventually, cut off from distractions, Ryan gets down to the pile.

He sets an alarm every day that signals the need to start one hard task—opening a file he has been avoiding or making a feared phone call. When that alarm goes off, don't stop to think! Just act. Open the file, dial the number. Small, starting steps. Everything else will follow.

I've pressed him to keep an appointment book that includes the times he is pledged to whittle away at his to-do list and suggested he honor those appointments as he would any other. To date, he has researched and purchased a magnificent palm pilot, but it sucks him into its glamorous gadgets at least as often as it keeps him on track. He has faith, though, in its future powers to support his need for structure.

Each of these techniques is a tried-and-true method for overcoming procrastination and getting yourself down to business. (There are lots more available in any book on procrastination, if avoidance is one of your big issues.) Ah, but what makes Ryan actually use the techniques? Well, he has faced what hurts — namely, that he's been wallowing in a work life where he *could* succeed and very few of us like ourselves better for wallowing.

In addition, Ryan has let go of his fantasy of leaving the business, and that awakening to hard reality, after a harsh bump, has had a motivating effect. He replaced the fantasy of leaving with a vision of himself as a corporate president, and you know what? He likes that mental picture. It gets him going, where escapist fantasies only kept him stuck and stoned.

Finally, his look back at his own patterns has helped Ryan appreciate the rebel he's been and perhaps no longer needs to be. The courage to tolerate this kind of self-awareness made his reluctance to dive into the pile a lesser demon. A demon still, but one that can be faced. The more Ryan eats through his pile, the better, more effective, more competent he feels about himself. The better he feels, the more likely he is to do the hard thing again tomorrow. He has set himself in motion.

James and Mai have worked long enough in couples therapy to broach their taboo topics. James has stepped onto uncomfortable ice, expressing his pain and disappointment over Mai's sexual rejection. Mai has begun to respond, venting long-buried anger and eventually, hesitantly, wishing for a closer, more connected marriage. The problem, she explains, is that she's been shut down for so long that the very idea of opening up physically makes her shudder.

Should even sex require discipline? Frankly, sometimes yes.

Coming out of a physically withdrawn comfort zone to risk sexual intimacy is an awkward and fearful process. One of the main principles of discipline, you'll recall, is that you don't always act according to your feelings. Be guided by your best judgment, even when your feelings may be moaning "No no, I don't wanna."

When what you've been avoiding is obviously unpleasant—a confrontation with your teenager, getting on the scale after the holidays, your financial reckoning—it's easy to see why discipline requires that you act according to what is best or right, despite your bad feelings. This rule gets a lot trickier to grasp when the actions you are avoiding are presumably positive, not to mention urgently desirable. Mai has been waiting to desire physical closeness before she will bring herself to reach out. She, and James, have been waiting a long time.

What I know, though Mai does not yet believe it, is that feelings result from actions as often as action follows feeling. If Mai allows herself to be physically close, awful and awkward though it will be initially, desire and delight may eventually reassert themselves. At first she will be in the grip of a cold anxiety, stiff and reluctant in his arms. But if they proceed, slowly and deliberately, if James is patient and Mai is willing to endure the discomfort, together they may rediscover pleasure. And that will go a long way toward healing the emotional breach.

The three of us map a slow program of physical connection, moving from hand-holding to eye contact and skin-to-skin embraces. Mai has decided she is willing to abandon her hermit shell, in part, I think, because if she and James are closer she won't have to come to therapy and talk about her feelings anymore. I'll take whatever motivation works, so James and I promise her that if they are able to reestablish a physical connection, to touch, hug, and kiss and maybe even make love occasionally, she never has to see me again. We laugh because it's true.

Such strategies for successfully navigating your tightrope work. The techniques suggested to help Ryan overcome procrastination, or James and Mai's slow program of sexual reconnection, or Lydia's determined step-by-step progress toward becoming a mother are each examples of time-tested strategies for tolerating discomfort.

Other people create absolutely original passages, with fear-reducing solutions I could never have envisioned. These novel strategies are executed by people freer to generate creative life solutions because they have faced what hurt, looked back to discover their own obstacles, and made a firm decision to move forward despite their anxiety.

Remember Ruth, who regained all that weight and hid out from men in the meantime? She restarted her diet during our work together, but that was clearly no panacea for the fear of rejection that got in her way the last time. The very prospect of personal ads, singles groups, or online dating overwhelmed her, and probably would no matter what the scale said. How to avoid another disappointing cycle?

Ruth came up with a marvelous back door to short-circuit her fear of rejection—a scheme to produce a bachelor-and-his-pet calendar as a fund-raiser for her favorite charity. Seems Ruth sits on the board of a pet adoption support group for strays. The group needed community visibility and an income source; Ruth needed to meet men in a less scary way, and voilà!

Ruth is producing the calendar, calling to meet every bachelor who interests her. Sometimes she feels her interviews require several meetings, you know, so she can get the pet's history just right. So far no man has turned down the possibility of being included in a calendar with Fido. Ruth is having such a good time being sought after, she's thinking of a follow-up hunks-of-the-

Delaware-Valley little black book. Not bad for a chubby, depressed, middle-aged couch potato, wouldn't you say?

So, if you are, at this moment, your own version of a chubby, depressed baked potato,

if you are suffering through your life until something or someone puts it out of its misery,

if you are restless, unfocused, and stale,

if you know your next step but you are fighting it, fearful of it,

if you are any of these things or any of the people you've been reading about to this point—

you know what you have to do. And now you know how to do it.

The Seventh Step: Taking Action

Prepare yourself for the paradox of change. From a distance it is a yellow brick road to your heart's desire. Close in on it, though, and its costs will suddenly magnify a hundredfold in your imagination. However unsatisfying your comfort zone, remember that it is safe, if only by virtue of its utter familiarity. Challenge that safety and in the days and weeks preceding your departure, what was painful or unsatisfying may be cloaked in the sweet glow of home. At the very moment you approach its outer boundaries, comfort is apt to exercise its full gravitational pull.

By comparison, what's new will seem at best an awkward fit. After all, if you are going someplace you've never been, by definition you'll have to take a road you've never traveled. It can't feel as safe as the roads you've known. But it will get you where you are hoping to go after you've won the fight with yourself.

I must acknowledge, however, that on the way there you might spend some time feeling sick at heart. Some change does not feel merely temporarily unsafe; it feels damn near unendurable. You will not be protected from that tide of anguish simply because you chose to do the letting go. On the contrary, a loss over which you have no control may eventually awaken the pain-numbing acceptance of the inevitable. Self-propelled change, on the other hand, is your full and certain responsibility and comes without benefit of anesthesia. It hurts as long as it hurts. And while it hurts, you will suffer.

Perhaps you are on that killer roller-coaster ride right now, as you are reading this. Or maybe you are just at the border of your comfort zone, hesitating because you know how it's going to feel out there, and the prospect of so much pain frightens you. Or you got out there and it was so tough to take you fled back to the old familiar platform, where you're not happy but you're not hurting either. That's OK. Some of us need several tries before we make it across the tightrope.

Here's the one thing I know to be true, and so do you, though your knowledge may be temporarily drowned out by the clamor of your feelings: *Pain passes*. Those who stand and face pain will still be standing when it passes—but in a better place. Use everything you've learned about challenging your comfort zone, and I promise, you will find yourself among the standing.

Here is what I hope I've emphasized enough: that every nibble is a forward step. That the new becomes cozy and safe and familiar only by trying it on, by wearing it for some little while. Keep in mind poet Jack Kerouac's caution: "Walking on water wasn't built in a day." Give yourself sufficient time to cross your tightrope at your own pace. When you do take that awful step into the cold, believe that you will come to tolerate, then relish, finally glory in your next destination. Because you will, you know, and it will be worth it.

Remember that your next step may be a step inside, challenging your comfortable view of yourself or your world. You may stay in the same outer circumstances yet profoundly change your experience of them. Spiritual transformation and psychological maturation are paths in themselves, requiring their own kind of courage to get you to that next higher platform.

You may be one of those people who cannot identify that next comfortable platform, whether the change is spiritual or concrete. From the vantage of your current comfort zone, you may be unable to envision any new objective at all. And whatever you do imagine will surely turn out very differently once you get there. You may have to leap into midair and trust to the currents. Don't use the absence of a clear objective as permission to go nowhere.

Remember, we are all fighting inertia. The laws of physics are the laws of the psychological universe, as well. A body in motion tends to stay in motion. A body at rest tends to stay at rest. In your comfort zone, you are a body at rest. You need to set yourself into motion.

Can a stationary pendulum start itself swinging? Hmmm, no, it requires the movement of the earth around it. But a human can, because we were endowed with an internal energy that the pendulum lacks. We have spirit, soul, will. We can initiate our own action. From rest we can begin movement, minuscule perhaps, but motion. And from that motion, in wider and wider circles, we push at our boundaries, set ourselves on a fresh course. We gather energy, stir motion. But we start it in small swings of our internal pendulum.

Don't necessarily think of changing your life. That may be too huge, too overwhelming. Cut it down to size. Think of changing your view instead, or refreshing your brain, stimulating your perspective. Neuroscientists say we ward off the mental deterioration of aging by solving new problems, seeing new sights, simply driving new streets. Certainly one could ward off a stale soul by doing the same.

So many actions, small and grand, may jolt your spirit awake, straighten your spine, stiffen your nerve. If you don't know your direction, your vision, your goal, then spend some time doing what is new or different or strange. Chances are great a new direction will find you, but you must gather the will to turn an inch from your old one.

Whether or not you know your next step, use this Buddhist parable as a guide and inspiration, reminding you to make that small turn toward the new:

> *An enemy shoots an arrow at your heart. It falls short and lays at your feet. Now you have two choices. You can finish the job, or you can turn and walk away.*

Fear is the poison in that arrow—fear, uncertainty, guilt, shame, worry, rage, rejection, and self-defeat. And the shooter is surely someone or some situation to whom you are profoundly attached, whether your lover, your job, your parent, your unfulfilled ambition, or your own self-limiting beliefs. Resist your impulse to rush forward and clutch the old familiar arrow. Turn, turn, if only just to look over your shoulder, if only just to imagine a gate.

Wrench yourself away from the arrow—take one step, and watch and wait and walk a little farther. Look away from the arrow and take the leap toward faith and eventually a new path will appear. When it does, don't be surprised to discover that the path's not new at all; it was there all along. It just takes most of us time to see it.

Some may arrive at a new comfort zone with no one critical turn in the path. Instead, they evolve in a new direction, speaking up more and more in a partnership until the balance of power shifts in their favor, shouldering more and more of the leadership until they find themselves captain, continuously pressing themselves forward into the unknown. That's a nice way to live. Maybe it's even the ideal. But it's not most of us, and it doesn't have to be.

The rest of us move forward in fits and jerks, happily hibernating bears who stay in a cave until some serious weather change forces us outside. We speak about the importance of challenging ourselves, but we lie down until the urge passes. We recommend a life lived at the fulfilling edge, but we settle into the fat middle.

I hope I've made it clear that there is nothing wrong with the fat middle. In fact, it's a perfectly delicious place to be, for some time. But it is too easy to get stuck there, to linger, even to wallow, long after that time is up.

If you find yourself there, and especially if you are lying limp, without the catalyst of searing pain to get you mobilized, you will need to force march yourself through the seven steps described here. You are not savoring your life, you are only surviving it, and alternate action might not even occur to you. Your horse is still standing, but it's not going anywhere.

You are the person in the dreary job that pays the bills, who as yet cannot imagine what else to do. You are the person in the decaying marriage, lonely, numb, or resentful, but absent the infidelity or abuse that might more easily galvanize you into action. Your clients underpay, but at least there's cash coming in. Your family life, your friendship circle, your financial status is just OK, but the path to splendid is invisible from where you are squatting.

The thing is, you are us. All of us, at least at one time or another. The magnetic power of the comfort zone is such that few of us escape its pull. We all linger, complaining, confused, or deadened. We are waiting, without necessarily knowing we are waiting. Waiting for an emotional earthquake, for rescue, for relief. We are waiting for something to happen, despising the truth that requires so much from us—that *we* are the something that has to happen.

In March of 2002, a one-thousand-pound cow escaped a slaughterhouse by jumping a ten-foot fence. The cow then enjoyed the Ohio countryside for eleven days, until animal control personnel were able to recapture her. When they did, the Cincinnati Reds awarded the cow the keys to the city, and she was retired to live out her days at an animal preserve. Accepting those keys on behalf of the cow, the artist Peter Max said, "After all, at one time or another we have all leapt some ten-foot wall."

Have we? What about you?

INDEX

Excess Baggage
Getting Out of Your Own Way
by Judith Sills, Ph.D.

Are you standing in the way of your own happiness?

Maybe you always have to finish what you start—from a book to a dismal marriage. Or your mother is always there when you need her—but sometimes you wish she had somewhere else to go. Each of us has a little too much of our own good thing; it's excess baggage that's holding us back.

As Judith Sills points out in this exceptionally wise and refreshingly pragmatic book, *everyone* has baggage. It's the aspect of your personality that keeps getting in your way.

Excess Baggage shines a light on our blind spots, defining five common obstacles to finding our happiness:

- We need to be right

- We feel superior

- We dread rejection

- We create drama

- We cherish our anger

Life doesn't have to be so hard. Using easy-to-follow but powerful psychological exercises, Dr. Sills helps you discover just what it is about yourself that keeps you from getting what you want. Then you can set your excess baggage down forever—and get out of your own way.

ISBN 0-14-200419-7